M000206033

"Tim Kelton is the epitome of a pastor: kind, gentle, caring and committed. Committed to serving God and the people of the community he lives in. As our friendship has grown, I now realize these qualities were formed out of his own physical struggles. He has a sweet spirit that comes through on the pages of his book; God In You Can Change The World."

Stephen J. Campbell, President,
Campbell Financial Services, Fishersville, Va.

"Comedy and drama are woven through everyone's life, however, only a few are able to communicate the ups and downs through the gift of storytelling and honor God in the process! Tim Kelton is one of those few."

Cosette Conaway, Pastor, The Lighthouse,
A Foursquare Gospel Church, Lynchburg, Va.

"The lifetime ministry of Tim Kelton has blessed those who know him. I am sure that God In You Can Change The World will have an impact on your life."

Durwood Cowan, Pastor,
Harriston Christian Center, Harriston, Va.

From The Heart

GOD IN YOU CAN CHANGE THE WORLD

NEVER FORGET HOW MUCH
THE GOD OF THE BIBLE
LOVES YOU!

Tim Ketto

HEBREWS 13:8 - JUNE 2007

From The Heart

GOD IN YOU CAN CHANGE THE WORLD

Tim Kelton

TATE PUBLISHING & *Enterprises*

 TATE PUBLISHING
& Enterprises

Tate Publishing is committed to excellence in the publishing industry. Our staff of highly trained professionals, including editors, graphic designers, and marketing personnel, work together to produce the very finest books available. The company reflects the philosophy established by the founders, based on Psalms 68:11,

"THE LORD GAVE THE WORD AND GREAT WAS THE COMPANY OF THOSE WHO PUBLISHED IT."

If you would like further information, please contact us:

1.888.361.9473 | www.tatepublishing.com

TATE PUBLISHING & Enterprises, LLC | 127 E. Trade Center Terrace

Mustang, Oklahoma 73064 USA

From the Heart: God in You Can Change the World

Copyright © 2007 by Tim Kelton.

This title is also available as a Tate Out Loud audio product.

Visit www.tatepublishing.com for more information.

No part of this publication may be reproduced, stored in a retrieval system or transmitted in any way by any means, electronic, mechanical, photocopy, recording or otherwise without the prior permission of the author except as provided by USA copyright law.

All Scripture quotations are taken from The New King James Version / Thomas Nelson Publishers, Nashville: Thomas Nelson Publishers. Copyright © 1982. Used by permission. All rights reserved.

The opinions expressed by the author are not necessarily those of Tate Publishing, LLC.

Book design copyright © 2007 by Tate Publishing, LLC. All rights reserved.

Cover design and Interior design by Jennifer Redden

Cover Photography by Angela Beadles

Cover Photo of Author's hands–2007, holding his 1960's bible

Published in the United States of America

ISBN: 978-1-6024700-4-X
07.04.10

In Loving Memory

"Honor your father and your mother,
that your days may be long upon the land
which the Lord your God is giving you."
Exodus 20:12

~

Frank Kelton
Born in Chester, Arkansas
January 11, 1911–September 26, 1955

Claude Earl Fannin
Born in Elliotville, Kentucky
August 10, 1916–July 8, 1994

Mary Maxine (Maddy) Fannin
Born in New Castle, Indiana
June 4, 1921–March 20, 1996

Myda Norine (Falls) Kelton
Born in Lamar, Missouri
March 30, 1914–March 17, 2006

~

"For with God nothing will be impossible."
Luke 1:37

Marquita Norine (Kelton) Clevenger
Born in Carthage, Missouri
May 10, 1936–May 13, 2003

This book is dedicated to my faithful and discerning bride of over thirty-seven years, Claudia Sue Fannin Kelton. Her insights and spiritual strength have brought me both significant peace and great joy as a man committed to the awesome God of the Bible. From the first moment my eyes fell upon her, I knew she was the one that God had prepared for me.

Acknowledgements

Tate Publishing Company, Mustang, Oklahoma. Thank you for not only allowing an unknown author as myself to have the great privilege of writing and publishing this book but also surrounding me with your Godly advice and expertise in the writing, editing and publishing process. You have truly demonstrated Christian love, wisdom and integrity.

Siblings. To have the love and respect of my sister and brothers has both comforted and strengthened me over the years of my life. Please receive my heartfelt gratitude: David Kelton and wife Brinda; Nathan Kelton and wife Donna; my sister Marquita (now home with the Lord) and her husband Duane Clevenger; and my brother-in-law Larry Fannin and his wife Sun.

Maranatha! Foursquare Church, Stuarts Draft, Virginia. A heartfelt thanks for the loving and prayerful support from each of these members and spiritual leaders throughout the Shenandoah Valley: *(alphabetical order)* Bucky Allen & Judy Campbell, Richard & Angela Beadles, Chester & Shannon Burke, Charles & Grace Campbell, Timmy & Tiffany Campbell, Roger & Debbie Carter, Al & Beth Grimm, Lita Hunt, Pat Johns, Jonathan & Katie Kelton, Jeremy & Valerie Kong, Troy & Melissa Lewis, Eric & Arlene Rakes, Ruby Rankin, Ramona Sanchez, David & Shelby Segan, Charles & Susan Sprouse, Bob & Linda Swartz; *(Future "Little Church" Leaders):* Courtney Beadles, Rose Benson, Kady Campbell, Caleb Kong, Jillian Lewis and Mazie Lewis.

International Foursquare Church, Los Angeles, California. I am forever indebted for the faith, trust and respect that has been shown to me over the past thirty-six years in the ministry. A special word of gratitude to the *Foursquare leaders in Virginia* that have so often encouraged me: Pastor Cosette Conaway and the Lighthouse Foursquare Church family, Lynchburg; Pastors Hunter & Mary Phillips and the Foursquare Church family, Lexington; Pastors Andy & Brenda Salcedo and the New Life Foursquare Church family, Staunton; Pastors Bob & Vicki Smith and Pastors Scott & Kyle Jungers and the Foursquare Family Life Center, Richmond.

Fellow colleagues in Virginia. The depth of gratitude within my heart for both business and ministry friends that have strengthened and reinforced my life for many years is immense. A special "Thank You" to: David & Jo Anthony, Staunton; Dick Booth, Verona; Stephen Campbell, Fishersville; Pastors Jim & Sharon Chappell and the White Hill Church of the Brethren family, Stuarts Draft; Pastors Durwood & Judy Cowan and the Harriston Christian Center family, Weyers Cave; Gary Eavers, Stuarts Draft; Petie & Betty Eavers, Stuarts Draft; Charles & Leslie Wallace, Staunton.

New Life Radio, WNLR, *Churchville, Virginia.* It has been a great honor to be a part of one of the most influential voices for Christ within the Commonwealth of Virginia, situated in the heart of the Shenandoah Valley. After two separate opportunities as the "On Air" host of *The Sonrise Show* for nearly four years in the '80s as well as serving as host of *The Evening Show* for over three and a half years from 2002 thru 2005, I am eternally grateful. My heartfelt gratitude is extended to three deeply committed and dedicated Christian leaders and friends that helped to open such a wonderful season of ministry for me personally: Tom Watson, General Manager; Russ Whitesell, Program Director; and Nina Gross, Administrator.

Contents

Each Chapter Title in this book is also a "Sermon Title" from one of Tim Kelton's documented four-thousand past sermons.

Foreword

"To console those who mourn in Zion,
to give them beauty for ashes,
the oil of joy for mourning,
the garment of praise for the spirit of heaviness."
Isaiah 61:3

The life story of a faithful minister of the Gospel can be truly educational and inspiring. Educational in many ways, as we watch the minister serve and grow and sometimes struggle through the myriad aspects of ministry. Inspiring, when God rightly receives the glory for the successes and times of blessing. Inspiring, when we see the evidences of God's continued faithfulness to his servant.

True to their calling as God's servants, Tim and Claudia Kelton have shown great courage and integrity in living the Gospel as well as teaching it. As a fellow minister I have known them for 26 years, and I appreciate their devoted service to God and humanity. I am constantly inspired by God's faithfulness to the Kelton family, by their commitment to Him, and by their desire to continually wear the "garment of praise." Thank you, Tim, for sharing your life with us in the pages of this inspiring book, *From the Heart—God In You Can Change The World.*

Rev. Andrew Salcedo
Pastor, New Life Foursquare Gospel Church, Staunton, Virginia.

Preface

When Tim Kelton is asked about his age, his usual reply is, "Do you mean my age in years or my age in mileage?" It was in the year 1956, at age eight, that he surrendered his young life to Christ during a special children's crusade within his home church, First Assembly of God, North Kansas City, Missouri. During a near death experience at Research Hospital in Kansas City, Missouri, God called him to become a "preacher" at age nine. That decision as a young boy defied the curse of three generations of "atheism" on his father's side of the family as well as generations of "witchcraft" on his mother's side of the family that preceded him. He preached his first sermon at a David Wilkerson *Teen Challenge* street meeting in Harlem, New York, at age seventeen.[1]

Tim was twenty-one when he married his sweetheart and partner for life, Claudia Sue Fannin, in the summer of 1969. They met while preparing their lives for ministry at Mount Vernon Bible College, situated in a rural community between Columbus and Cleveland, Ohio.[2]

Tim received his first pastoral assignment to reopen the closed First Foursquare Gospel Church in Charlotte, North Carolina, at age twenty-two. He was "ordained" at age twenty-three at Angeles Temple, in Los Angeles, California, the headquarters church for the International Church of the Foursquare Gospel.[3]

At age twenty-five, Tim was the original television host of the *Trinity Broadcasting Praise The Lord Show,* laying the seed for the nationally acclaimed *PTL Club.*[4] Little did he fully understand that his life, along with hundreds of others at that time, would help establish Christian television for decades to follow within the city of Charlotte, North Carolina, that would continually reach out not only to America but to other nations around the world.[5]

Tim invited John Giminez, pastor of Rock Church, at Virginia Beach, Virginia, to participate in the Third Pioneer Pastor's Seminar conducted at Tim and Claudia's church in Charlotte. Just as Pastor Giminez and Tim were preparing to enter the sanctuary for ministry to pastor's from all across the southeast, John Giminez put his finger on Tim's chest and softly communicated his desire that both Tim and Claudia should attend another pastor's conference.[6] This invitation was to Bethesda Missionary Temple, located in the heart of Detroit, Michigan.

Tim and Claudia had entered the 3,000-seat sanctuary of this large church in Detroit, and were seated on the back row. The guest speaker from California stopped in the middle of his message, with apologies to the large crowd for his interruption, and pointed out Tim and Claudia while asking them to stand to their feet. He spoke to them publicly about their future and then asked them to make their way to the front of the sanctuary for prayer. The pastor, James Beall, asked his mother, the founding pastor of that church, to lay her prayerful hands upon Tim and Claudia. Tim was twenty-seven at that historic moment that greatly impacted his life.

At age twenty-eight he submitted to an invitation to join with the popular Christian Latin singing group The Amigo's for ten days of ministry in Guatemala, ninety days after the 7.5 killer earthquake there that took the lives of more than twenty-two thousand people. Tim preached to the largest crowds that he had ever stood before at the 2,000-member Prince Of Peace Church, situated in the heart of the capitol, Guatemala City.[7]

At age twenty-nine, he stood alongside his older brother David Kelton on the platform of the 5,000-member congregation of Rex Humbard's Cathedral of Tomorrow, in Cuyahoga Falls, Ohio.[8] Together, they shared David's powerful testimony of deliverance and freedom from six-teen years of addictions to alcohol and drugs.[9] They had been invited to participate in this Operation Motivation Day, along with guest's author Ann Kiemel and Pastor Tommy Barnett.

During the year of 1979, at age thirty-one, he completed two separate journeys, totaling in thirty-seven days of ministry, to both The Philippine Islands and South Korea. Tim was privileged to minister in those two nations' federal prisons. He was flown to three separate Philippine islands as well as the Capitol City, Manila, to lead in ministry conferences.[10] Tim's sixteen days in South Korea included ministry at one of the largest Christian high schools in South Korea, which was greatly influencing the Buddhist culture of that nation for Christ.[11]

His feet stepped on to the soil of the South Pacific island of Papua New Guinea as Field Director and missionary at age thirty-three.[12] Surviving a near fatal auto accident on a jungle road as well as numerous threats on his life, he still helped to release that Papua New Guinean church to fulfill its destiny of leading itself. At age thirty-five, he had completed his second ministry tour in Australia, touching such major cities as Sydney, Perth and Adelaide.

Physicians at the University of Virginia Medical Center in Charlottesville, Virginia, collectively voiced their medical opinion that Tim was in the final ninety days of his life due to his contracting a deadly vascular disease complicated by malignant malaria that had struck him while in the jungles of Papua New Guinea. That dark and significant day in his life was the day before Thanksgiving, 1986.[13] Tim was only thirty-eight. Yet today, at the completion and publishing of this, his first book, he is fifty-eight.

While documenting so many wonderful opportunities for ministry within his life, Tim Kelton has many regrets. He openly shares numerous stories from his heart. Stories of success and failure, right decisions and wrong decisions, seasons of hope coupled with times of deep discouragement and sorrow. He is quick to communicate his personal amazement and bewilderment in how the God of the Bible would use a *nobody* like himself.

Preaching more than 4,000 sermons, with ministry in nearly 150 towns and cities, in 14 U.S. states and 9 nations, including two years walking along jungle trails, today his body is very fragile. With a marked curvature of his shoulders and weakness in his lower legs, many are the times that he walks with his wooden cane for added strength. Now in his eleventh year as pastor of Maranatha! Foursquare Church, Stuarts Draft, Virginia, he sits in a chair to deliver his Sunday sermons, unable to stand for long periods of time. However, he remains full of thanksgiving and joy as he celebrates more than thirty-six ministry years spanning four decades.

Some people may judge Tim Kelton as a *nobody,* but his life is a testimony to the grace, compassion and mercy of the awesome God. With deep passion comes the purpose for the writing of this particular book, hoping to convey to the heart of every reader that even if you are perceived as a *nobody,* if you will surrender your life and destiny to the God of the Bible for His purposes and goals, then in time, *God in you can change the world!*

"For you see your calling, brethren,
that not many wise according to the flesh,
not many mighty, not many noble, are called.
But God has chosen the foolish things
of the world to put to shame the wise,
and God has chosen the weak things
of the world to put to shame
the things which are mighty;
and the base things of the world
and the things which are despised
God has chosen,
and the things which are not,
to bring to nothing the things that are,
that no flesh should glory in His presence."
I Corinthians 1:26–29

Introduction

The true stories that you are about to read are not intended to impress or amaze the reader with the talents of the author. These are only a few of the stories *from the heart* of a man that has endeavored to surrender his life to God since childhood. The objective of this book is to challenge every reader with the reality that the Living God of the Bible desires to touch our dark world with the Light of the Good News through His people.

Please note that the name satan and related names are not capitalized within the pages of this book. This was the author's decision and his desire to not acknowledge satan in this manner even to the point of violating grammatical rules. Also, please note that some names have been changed in order to preserve the privacy of certain individuals while maintaining the integrity and purpose of this book.

So fasten your seat belt! You are about to enter into an adventure of a lifetime. You will laugh and you will cry. You will moan and sometimes just be silent. This is an opportunity for you to be challenged *to change your world!*

Chapter 1

GOD KNOWS WHERE YOU ARE

"You, O Lord, remain forever;
Your throne from generation to generation."
Lamentations 5:19

Most people that I have met over the years have at least some interest in their family history; inwardly pondering about their roots and heritage. Wondering about such things as, "Was there anyone famous or maybe notorious within my family background?" How about such hopeful thoughts as, "Maybe one of my ancestors was a millionaire and left an undiscovered inheritance for future generations? Oh, please let that be so!" Unfortunately, for a lot of us, our undiscovered inheritance was not a million dollars, but rather, a few or maybe more than a few unwanted and unsolicited sad and depressing stories about our family's history.

Many of us have questioned, "Why couldn't my family have been a "good" family to be born in to, instead of a family of disappointments and bitter failures? A family of happiness and joyfulness instead of a legacy filled with dark shadows and sorrow? A family of peace, instead of a family filled with chaos and madness that we are forced to live with everyday?" Sometimes wondering how our lives would have been different "if only!"

I am here to tell you that there is hope! I don't care what your family heritage is; there is a real possibility that your particular life can break free from those depressing shadows! It won't be easy. You will have to "wage war" for the freedom that you are hoping for, but it is achievable, *"For with God* (The God of the Bible) *nothing will be impossible"* (Luke 1:37).

I was devastated as a young teenager when I began to comprehend my family history. My Father, Frank Kelton, had been raised in the hills of Arkansas as a "third generation" atheist. He and his brothers were taught that there was no God. They were to only trust in what they could see with their eyes and touch with their hands. They were told to beware of "preachers and churches"; they only want your money. Tragically, for some of those men, three generations of that ancestral teaching left a legacy of addictions to alcohol, gambling and sexual perversion.

My Mother, Myda Falls Kelton, had been raised believing in God. However, the history of her family was also distressing. I was stunned to hear the stories of "witchcraft" being practiced during Friday night séances' by several of my great aunts. Shamefully, the legacy of a family that was considered to be a very religious family left its treacherous affect and ugly stain of sexual impurity, adultery and broken marriages on many generations that followed.

There is a Scripture verse that has continually stood as a warning to me personally while at the same time has given me hope as I have embraced it very tightly during the years of my life. It is a clear and powerful "Word from God," the God of the Bible, to all of us who will have an ear to hear it.

> "For I, the Lord your God, am a jealous God, visiting the iniquity of the fathers upon the children to the third and fourth generations of those who hate Me, but SHOWING

MERCY to thousands, to those who love Me and keep My commandments" (Exodus 20:5,6).

How my mother and father got together is still mind-boggling to me. She had experienced a remarkable conversion to Christ as a youth. As a result, she declared that she was called to be a missionary to the continent of Africa. Dad was raised as an atheist. Mom graduated as "valedictorian" of her senior class in high school. Dad didn't finish high school. Yet they found each other, fell in love and were married. End of story, right? No. Many were the occasions that they clashed. By that I mean Mom's faith in God clashing with Dad's faith in man. Yet remarkably their mutual deep love for each other held them together.

The Bible says, *"And we know that all things work together for good to those who love God, to those who are the called according to His purpose"* (Romans 8:28). I am so grateful for this promise of hope. As I have witnessed in my family many times, you don't always see the result that you were hoping for, but you can experience the peace that comes when you realize that the God of the Bible is watching over your life with the purpose of bringing about *"good."*

One of the most remarkable stories that I have ever heard was about my only sister, Marquita, the first-born child of Frank and Myda Kelton. She was born without eyes. My parents were devastated. Every physician sadly expressed that there was nothing that could be done to reverse this tragic dilemma. No medical procedure could fill those two empty eye sockets.

My desperate atheist father, accompanied by my mother's Christian father, Fred Falls, took this newborn infant to be prayed for. There were no immediate results. After returning home, Dad brought his only child to Mom's bedside, telling her that the special prayers didn't work. However, in the seventh week of my sister's life, a "miracle" came to my family.

While Mom was bathing Marquita on our small kitchen table, her eyelids both opened with sparkling new eyes. There were no empty eye sockets. Mom quickly picked up her little baby girl and made her way to the back door, emotionally screaming to gain the attention of her father, Fred Falls, who was working out in the garden. When he frantically made his way to where this weeping mother was standing with her baby and saw those two miracle eyes, he fell to his knees, also weeping and praising God.

When my dad made his way home from his job and held his baby girl in his arms, he was to be forever changed. While this young father did not accept Christ into his life at that historic moment, he could no longer deny the reality of God.

When my parents hurriedly carried their child to the doctor, even the medical staff broke into emotional tears. The physician took Marquita into his arms, speaking to my parents with firm conviction that only God could bring about such a miracle.

He then confessed to them that he had grown cold toward God over the years of his life. He had been too busy with his medical career to remember his own spiritual roots. However, that day he expressed his desire to once again draw close to God.

It was an astonishing moment, and only a short time from that day of meeting with my parents, they were informed that this physician had unexpectedly died. My mother always believed that the traumatic seven weeks that she endured with her first-born child and her empty eye sockets was part of God's plan in her life. A plan to reach into the hearts of two special men and show them their desperate need for change.

Nearly a decade had passed since that miracle day when Dad had been arrested along with several other men that he worked with. They had been charged with stealing from the company that they worked for. It was another devastating moment for my family. Mom was overwhelmed and confused and couldn't stop weeping. All of those prayers that she had prayed for her husband's salvation now seemed totally lost.

Several of the men from our small Assembly of God Church visited Dad at the jail. Long story short, as some say, they actually offered the title deeds on their homes as surety for Dad's bail and release. He was released and eventually made his way back to freedom from jail.

However, he was deeply marked by the act of love of those church members. He was overwhelmed by the reality that people he did not know personally would place themselves in such potential risk. What he didn't clearly understand at that moment was that this church family, along with my mother, had been interceding on his behalf for many years. That man that had been a *third generation atheist* ultimately made his way to that small church sanctuary and surrendered his life to the God of the Bible.

The year of Dad's conversion to Christ was also the year that I was born. My most profound memory of him was a historic day within my own life. I wasn't old enough to go to school, but the memory of that day will always remind me of how much God loves me.

I was playing in the sand and gravel at the edge of our driveway when my young eyes focused upon that glistening brown copperhead snake that had worked its way to where I was sitting. I started screaming from fear as that snake began raising his head toward me. I can still see those beady eyes and forked tongue. I was screaming but frozen from fear, when my dad had hurriedly made his way from the garden toward the sound of his hysterical child. As I turned my eyes toward this frightened father, I saw him release his four-prong garden spade in the air. It was like watching someone throw a spear at a target.

Well, that garden spade struck that copperhead snake. How one of those four steel points struck that snake from the distance that Dad had thrown it could only be by the hand of a protecting angel. That snake was severed in half, but I was now even more hysterical.

Both halves of that snake took off in two different directions. Thankfully my dad swept me up into his strong arms and rushed me to the arms of my mother. Then he and my older brother David began their search for those two writhing and bloody snakes.

Dad and David made their way to the front porch where Mom was still trying to settle me down. Dad lifted the shiny lid to that paint can and slowly showed me what was left of that dead copperhead snake lying lifeless at the bottom. It still didn't bring me that much peace.

Then Dad asked Mom if I could go with him and David to the small creek about a mile away from our home. I remember Mom wasn't too happy about the situation as she reluctantly and tearfully released me into the strong arms of my dad.

We then climbed into Dad's old pickup truck and drove to the bridge overlooking the creek. Dad then hammered that shiny paint can lid tighter with his hammer and tossed it into the running water. The picture was clear to that young boy. That snake was dead and sealed in that old paint can and now floating downstream away from *me!*

I only have a few other memories of my dad. One of my best was when he was holding me in his strong arms after visiting a local ice cream parlor, and we were taking turns licking the ice cream cone. Another was when he had led me down the old, creaky, wooden floors of a small rural grocery store, then reached into an icebox cooler and pulled out two bottles of "Dad's Root Beer." Oh, and the time that he picked me up by my shirt collar and carried me down the hallway to my bed for punishment as a result of me throwing a rock in anger at my younger brother Nathan. It missed him, but it sure didn't miss that big living room window that was shattered and all over the place.

Another significant memory of Dad was that he was always kissing Mom. It was so embarrassing to us boys. They were kissing in the hallway, the kitchen, the living room, on the front porch, out in the yard and in the garden. Even our neighborhood friends would ask us why our mom and dad were always kissing. We just kept trying to ignore their "silly" kissing.

The most tearful memory that marked me for life was the day that I was escorted into our pastor's home and saw my mother laying on their sofa. Her face was swollen and covered with tears as she told us three sons that our father had died that afternoon while on the job. He died unexpectedly of a massive heart attack. All I could do was tearfully stare at her lips while thinking that Dad would never kiss them again. I was only seven years old. My younger brother Nathan was almost five and my older brother, David, was fourteen. My sister Marquita had just married Duane Clevenger the year before.

I remember that day like it was just yesterday. We as a family were huddled in the funeral car as we were following the hearse en-route to the cemetery. I remember saying to Mom, "This is Daddy's last ride, isn't it?"

Mom tearfully squeezed my hand. Our family was beleaguered by the early and unexpected death of forty-four year-old Frank Kelton. Through God's mercy, we found as much peace as is possible in the midst of this horrendous storm.

However, my sister Marquita, in the midst of her grieving over the loss of her dad, was becoming bitter toward God. Her inner feelings echoed the sentiments of many people that have lost a loved one. The question "Why?" is usually the first among many. "Why now, just when I've been married and started my own life? Why my family? My mother is now left with three young boys and no income to take care of them." Her heart was grieving over all of the loss that she and her family were experiencing, and her spirit was seething more bitterly toward God each day that passed.

Then it happened. Several months after Dad's death, Marquita was totally changed by a dream that horrified her. She was standing alone facing a police car with flashing lights on top. Two police officers were standing near the police car with Dad standing handcuffed between them. The officers were preparing to place Dad in the back seat of their car, when Dad stopped and began communicating with Marquita.

"Why didn't you leave me where I was," he said with certain emotional pain in his voice?

"God knew what was best for me. Why didn't you leave me where I was?" Then the officers began to assist Dad into the patrol car.

Marquita awakened from her dream audibly weeping and

crying out to God to forgive her for the anger and bitterness that she exuded. She pulled her husband Duane out of the bed to join her on their knees in prayer in thanking God for saving her father from a life of sorrow. She was a changed woman after that night, thanking God many times for His hand upon her life.

The next year, at age eight, I was to be forever grateful to a young couple that would hold a children's crusade in our church. I was one of the most excited boys in church when it was announced that a brand new red *Schwin Bicycle* would be the grand prize for the child that would bring the most visitors to the crusade. You have to understand that I knew clearly that this was my chance to own a bicycle. After Dad's death, money was hard to come by in our family, and a bicycle was way down the list of things that we needed.

I have no idea how Mom had the extra money, but when she handed me not one but two rolls of pennies to entice my friends with, I didn't hesitate. I invited every friend, neighbor, school buddy and non-buddy to the children's crusade with the gift of one shiny penny and the promise that my mother would pick them up at their home. A penny in those days would buy a piece of sweet candy or delicious bubble gum. A nickel would buy five baseball cards with bubble gum all in one pack. Well, by week's end, I had successfully invited and brought over one hundred children to the crusade.

I remember standing on the platform of our church and that young couple awarding me that beautiful red *Schwin Bicycle*. I was the "king" and did I ever show off that bicycle in my neighborhood. I was up and down that road in front of my house over and over, and you could not get that smile off of my face. Of course in those days, the new rage, especially for boys, was

clipping baseball cards on the spokes of your bicycle. I had successfully clipped four top baseball players' cards to my bicycle
with clothespins. My bike sounded like a motorcycle moving up
and down the road, and I was all smiles. I only wish today that I
still had those two Mickey Mantle cards, as well as those Willie
Mays and Hank Aaron cards in my possession.

However, I do have Christ in my heart today, and I owe
much to that young couple and their tender and eloquent delivery of the Gospel message that touched my young and hurting
heart. I made a genuine and heartfelt confession of Jesus Christ
as my personal Savior that week. Since then my life has never
been the same.

In the not too distant future, I would be lying in critical condition at Research Hospital in Kansas City, Missouri, as a result
of a simple tonsillectomy. I remember the first time I tried to
swallow after the operation, and the immediate excruciating look
that I gave my mother. For the average child that faces the challenge of having their tonsils removed it is a painful but usually
short-lived event, followed by lots of ice cream as their reward.

I had only been home from the hospital for a few days when
it happened. Mom had been awakened in the middle of the night
from a burning sensation from her wedding ring. As she was
troubled by that occurrence, she then overheard a gurgling sound
coming from our small bedroom just down the hall. As she hurriedly made her way into the room, switching on the overhead
light, she was horrified at the sight of blood trickling out of my
mouth. Much of my pillow and bed sheet were wet with my
blood. She rushed to turn me on my stomach as she screamed to
awaken my brothers David and Nathan.

I know it sounds pretty hard to believe, especially in this day and age of trying to make an effective appointment with your doctor, but I remember lying on my doctor's lap in the rear seat of the car as Mom was anxiously driving us across town to the hospital. He had responded to her telephone call and had made his way to our home. He kept working with the continual blood flowing out of my mouth as he was trying to communicate peace to me. However, I knew that I was in serious trouble.

After many hours in the Emergency Room of the hospital, the wound in my throat just would not heal. I was literally bleeding to death. My tender but weary mother had given the physicians permission to inject me with a drug that had never been tried on humans. They were convinced that I was dying and this was their only hope. Mom related to me years later that her prayerful decision to allow them to try a new medicine that night was a desperate decision to prevent losing another member of her family.

I told her during my time of recovery about what had happened to me. "Mommy, He just stood over there by the wall and looked at me." She just stared at me. "Mommy, He never spoke out loud, but I heard Him say that I wasn't going to die. That I'm going to be okay."

My mother's eyes filled with tears. "Mommy, you know what else?" I said weakly yet with excitement. Mother just looked at me and said, "What, honey?" "Mommy, when I grow up, I am going to be a preacher!"

My mother's whole facial expression just froze. Was her little boy hallucinating or did he have a holy touch from heaven? Believe me, it was genuine. That night marked me for the rest of my life. I knew that the God of the Bible had touched my life. Instead of becoming a *fourth generation atheist,* I was now going to be entrusted to lead future generations in following Christ, but not without great personal cost.

Now another momentous day had come. I just could not believe that my mother would make such a decision. She had just told my younger brother Nathan and I that we were going to move from our home in Kansas City, Missouri, to Charlotte, North Carolina. We were stunned at such a thought. This was our home and the yard that we enjoyed playing in. This is where we had our friends and had gone to school. North Kansas City is where our dad was buried. How could our mother make such an earth-shattering decision for our family?

My Uncle Don had been appointed as the principal of a brand new private Christian school to be opened within the city of Charlotte. He had asked Mom to take the leadership over the school lunchroom. Since Dad's death, she had been working for several years as a cook in a local public school cafeteria in North Kansas City.

She told us that we would be gone for only "one year" and then we would come back home. She appealed to us to be willing to help Uncle Don start this Christian school. Nathan was ten, and I was twelve. What else can you say to your widow mother but "Okay?"

It was one of the most heart-wrenching days of my young life when my best friend Roger, who lived a block away from our home, met with me in order for us to say "good-bye" to each other. We had ridden our bicycles to our favorite spot, a hill overlooking our neighborhood. We just sat there on the seats of those two bicycles and remembered all the good times that we had enjoyed together in our young lives.

We both chuckled when we rehearsed the many "apple wars"

in our apple orchard that we had endured. We remembered the time that we learned that you never chase a skunk. Then we broke out in laughter when we remembered tying the tails of our two dogs together, and how much trouble we got into with our parents. The dogs barked and snipped at each other for about two blocks before we could finally catch up with them and untie the rope. Oh, and then we both grunted out loud when we rehearsed the day that we jumped into the creek down the road and tried wrestling that huge muddy turtle out of the water to the bank of the creek. Boy was that a foolish and colossal mistake! The turtle won that wrestling match.

Then the moment came. We shook hands and tearfully said "goodbye" to each other. Yes, boys do cry. When he took off down the hill, we were both crying. I just stayed there for a little while, wiping the tears and wondering if life would ever be the same after that day. Mom had us all packed up, and we began our journey to Charlotte, North Carolina, the next morning. I was to soon discover that our lives would be forever changed.

We never lived in Kansas City again. The Christian school did go on to become a major influence within the city of Charlotte, but my Uncle Don had stepped down from the leadership of the school after only one and half years. Mom made the decision to resign as well. However, she decided that, we would remain in Charlotte.

Charlotte, North Carolina was a growing, bustling city. Growing up in this city during the next six years would be significant for me. From age twelve upon our arrival and age eighteen upon my departure for Bible College would provide me with many opportunities for maturity. Unfortunately, there would be many opportunities for failure as well, but thankfully the God of the Bible would continually demonstrate His mercy and grace upon my young life.

Mom really struggled with finding a church home that she felt at peace in. We attended the First Assembly of God for a while, which was part of our spiritual roots. Then she moved us to the Missionary Alliance Church for a season. That's where my brother Nathan and I were both baptized in water. We then visited an independent church called Garr Memorial Church. Mom was sure that this was to be our new church home, a critical decision for sure.

Chapter 2

Positioned To Overcome

"Likewise you younger people, submit yourselves to your elders.
Yes, all of you be submissive to one another,
and be clothed with humility,
for 'God resists the proud, but gives grace to the humble'."
I Peter 5:5

It had been a hot summer day in New York City. I was seventeen years old. Our church youth group had traveled to the "Big Apple" for ten days of adventure and ministry: the New York World's Fair, the L.A. Dodgers versus the N.Y. Mets, Times Square, Fifth Avenue, Macy's, Empire State Building, Statue of Liberty, United Nations, Mama Leone's Italian Restaurant, and David Wilkerson's Teen Challenge Center in Brooklyn.

Our pastor, Alfred Garr Jr., had determined to expose us teens to the "real world," as he called it, while under the protection of strong leaders. Our youth pastor, Dave Wood, had his hands full but was energetically working side by side with several other men and women from our independent charismatic church, located in Charlotte, North Carolina. For me, it would be a life-changing ten days that would mark me for the rest of my life.

Those days in New York City did open my eyes to the "real world." It was my first time to see men kissing men and women fondling each other, and that was while we were handing out Christian tracts in Greenwich Village. I'll never forget how gorgeous the young prostitute looked from nearly a block away. When we made our way to where she was standing in order to give her a tract and talk with her about Jesus Christ, I was stunned in silence. I was standing next to her as one of our leaders was talking with her. There were several facial scars and bruises. Her eyes were sunk back in her head. In spite of her make-up and provocative clothing, she was old, wasted and ugly up close. When I heard her say that she was only sixteen years old, a year younger than me, tears welled up in my eyes.

I had seen the affects of alcohol in my own family, but had never imagined the magnitude of alcoholism and drug addiction within just one community. The lower end of Fifth Avenue, known as the "Bowery," was full of both men and women who were vagrants, sleeping on newspapers with their lives ravaged by their addictions. My hatred for alcohol and drugs was entrenched within me from that day until this day, decades later.

It was our final night of this life-changing journey. We were in the midst of an evangelistic street meeting in Harlem. Don Wilkerson, David Wilkerson's brother, as well as other Teen Challenge leaders, was leading us. We had set up a public address system along with several lights, all connected to car batteries encased in special wooden crates. After several loud and noisy songs from the curbside, several of us visiting teens were picked to share our personal testimonies. We were to each step up to the single microphone stand. I actually thought I was going to faint when I was tagged as the final youth to speak.

It was truly amazing to see hundreds of people just stop and listen. Many of them were amused, but it would help them pass the time on this sultry evening. The crowd had become so large that the traffic on this side street was being seriously affected. Horns were honking while numerous voices were sparring with each other. It was a very memorable sight.

As I listened to the other teens from our youth group share their testimonies of Christ's influence upon their lives, I became disheartened. I could not think of anything too bad that I had done in my young life to warrant anything worthy of all of these people listening to. I was frantic. The only thing I could think of was when I stole a nickel candy bar from the grocery store when I was about ten-years old. Please understand that I was not a thief, but after my dad's death, extra money for things like my favorite Three Musketeers candy bar was rare.

Mom was somewhere in the grocery store getting the necessities with the few dollars that she had in her purse. I kept circling around the huge display of candy bars on sale. It was like I could actually taste that smooth marshmallow filling covered with milk chocolate. I kept looking to see if anyone was watching me while I slowly and discreetly maneuvered my hand to the display of more candy bars that I ever knew existed in the world. I kept telling myself that no one will miss just one candy bar, and then I did it. I snatched that Three Musketeers candy bar and hurriedly slipped it in my pocket. My heart was pounding when I climbed in our green and white Chevrolet outside the grocery store. Mom asked me what was wrong as we were making our way home. How do you actually stutter through the single word "Nothing?"

When we arrived home, I hurriedly made my way up to our apple orchard behind our house. As I leaned my back to that apple tree, making sure that it was between me and those all-seeing eyes of my mother; I slowly pulled that candy bar out of my pocket. It was like Thanksgiving, Christmas, and my birthday all in one. I slowly slid down to where I was now seated on the ground while I meticulously unwrapped that prize candy bar. That first bite was the most delicious taste that I could ever remember. I slowly slurped that first sugary bite while I was smacking my lips in near euphoria. Then another succulent bite entered my mouth, and then another, and then … just as I was working on that final bite, it happened.

My stomach started growling, and then rolling, and then I got dizzy-headed. Before I could finish off that final bite of candy now stuck in my mouth, I started throwing up. I rolled over on the ground and heaved and heaved. There is just no way that one little boy could vomit that much. I was groaning and moaning and trying to call out to my mom for help when it hit me. "Oh no! God is going to kill me for stealing that candy bar."

I then started crying and telling God that I was sorry. "God! Please give me one more chance! I'll never steal anything again! I promise, God! Please don't kill me!"

All of a sudden I realized that I was not in our old apple orchard in Kansas City, Missouri, but was standing on the sidewalk in Harlem, New York City. I then looked out onto that crowded street and into the eyes of drug addicts, hookers and gang members. Sweat was now trickling on my forehead as I was thinking, "I can't tell this crowd my story of stealing a candy bar. They'll laugh me out of New York City." Then it occurred to me that I should just read the most well known Bible scripture on earth. Who could go wrong doing that?

While the other youth that had been selected to share their testimonies were speaking, the people now standing in the street kept looking at me. You might think it strange, but I kept having this feeling that they were thinking that this guy who is coming up last must really have some story to tell. I could almost hear their minds thinking, "We'll just hang around and hear what he has to say."

Well, the sweat was still trickling, and it was now my turn to step up to that microphone. As I nervously opened my little zipper Bible to the Gospel of John, shuffling the pages to find the third chapter and then running my shaking finger down to verse sixteen, I took a deep breath. I had no more than began reading, *"For God so loved the world ..."* when I heard a muffled exploding sound directly behind me. People everywhere jumped while some yelled. Then there was a second muffled explosion. The crowded street was now a picture of pandemonium. It had happened so fast. Then the third explosion took place when a paper grocery bag full of liquid ruptured on my chest while standing at the microphone. It was splattered all over me. It was dripping off of my eyelashes. It was up my nostrils and in my mouth. I then got sick at my stomach and nearly vomited when I realized that the liquid in that paper bag bomb was warm urine. The nausea was quickly replaced with anger and outrage. How could someone do this? We later learned that one of the street gangs had climbed up on the building directly over us and dropped these paper bag bombs on the street meeting.

Before I could make a move, Don Wilkerson firmly grabbed my elbow and said, "Young man, you finish what you were about to say. The devil is not going to win tonight."

I looked into his eyes and inwardly thought, "Sir, you don't understand. I don't have anything to say."

I then turned and looked back out over the crowd in the

street. They had quickly calmed back down when they realized that the exploding sounds were not life threatening. It was at that very moment that I sensed my very first quickening of the Holy Spirit. I calmly reopened my wet little Bible and began reading aloud, *"For God so loved the world that He gave His only begotten Son, that whoever believes in Him should not perish but have everlasting life."*

I then simply said, "I have not only never been drunk, but I haven't even tasted alcohol. I have never done drugs of any kind. I have never slept with a prostitute. But, in all of my goodness, I was still lost and without God, until I humbled myself and asked His Son, Jesus Christ, into my life." I then stepped away from the microphone. The street had fallen to silence. One of the Teen Challenge leaders stepped up to the microphone, extending an invitation to those who would desire to accept Christ into their lives. To all of our surprise and deep joy, many people knelt at the curbside that night. It was my first sermon. It was maybe my best sermon.

With a renewed sense of purpose, I focused on my final year at East Mecklenburg High School. I was doing a lot of reflecting during my senior year. The emotion of finally making it through high school mixed with the uncertainty about the future was sometimes very disturbing, especially for this eighteen-year-old.

I had not done all that well academically and was greatly disappointed that I had really never entered into the sports programs. All three of us Kelton boys were very gifted in baseball. I kept thinking about that special day back in the ninth grade while a student at Charlotte Christian High School, when Coach Wrigley informed me that a friend of his who was a sporting scout from a South Carolina College would be present during the afternoon practice. Coach asked me to remain at the plate for a dozen or two extra pitches during the routine batting practice. He had told me before that I was one of the most gifted young players that he had met who had a "natural eye" for hitting the baseball. There was a definite sense in his dialogue with me that I could have a future in the sport of baseball. That afternoon, several of my teammates kept running into the woods after my two-dozen or so home-run hits.

I know this may seem strange, but one of my best memories while a student at East Mecklenburg High School was that I had applied for and had been accepted as one of the Mecklenburg County student school bus drivers, and I was only in the tenth grade.

I can assure you that the training process was tough and very thorough. No student driver would be accepted that had any kind of negative record that pertained to driving or any other part of his or her young life. It was made very clear that even after you had been given the permit authorizing you to drive a school bus and you received any kind of driving violation or any other negative report against you, your permit would be immediately revoked and there would be no second opportunity.

The pay at that time for the few student drivers that had become a part of the program was only thirty dollars a month. The bright side of that one dollar and fifty cents a day was the privilege of having our own transportation to and from school, if you didn't mind commuting to high school every day while driving a big orange school bus full of boisterous kids. That was okay with me. However, I did become weary of dealing with those noisy kids two times each day and five days each week. I have to tell you that I was often distressed and shocked with all of the "unmentionables" that I would have to clean up many evenings when I would park the bus for the night. I remained a student driver for two years.

It was now late in the summer of 1966. Graduation from East Mecklenburg High School in Charlotte had taken place just a few months earlier. However, my graduation had been dismal for me because I had failed my senior English class. This particular class had been mostly committed to the study of literature. I obviously didn't do well in literature. As a result I was entangled in six weeks of summer school in order to get my high school diploma. Thankfully, I successfully made it through that grueling summer session and was now headed off to Bible College, hoping to fulfill my lifelong dream of becoming a preacher.

The North Carolina sun was shining down on my freshly washed olive green 1951 Chevrolet Coupe. Larry, one of my best friends in high school, had been encouraged by his dad to sell me this car of his for seventy-five dollars. His parents had just given him a much newer car for a graduation gift. Believe me, I was very appreciative for their generosity toward me.

I was sweating and smiling as I had just loaded my new footlocker chest in the trunk of my car. I had packed up most everything that I owned and had it all stuffed either in that chest or any other empty space I could find in the car. At the youthful age of only eighteen, I was nervous and exhausted but very excited about this new season in my life that was about to begin.

I didn't perceive it as a problem in that my fifty-two year-old, widowed mother, Myda Kelton, was determined to make the trip to college with me. She had been left with the unenviable task of raising three boys as a single parent, and believe me, we clearly understood how important this special lady was to us three boys who had grown up without our father. Now she was trying to cope with the emotion of letting go of another one of those boys.

Well, with everything packed in, Mom and I pulled out of the driveway and were headed off to college. I hadn't even driven one full block from our little house before she started crying. By the time that I had stopped at the gas station nearby and topped off my fuel tank; checked the oil level one more time, walked around the car kicking all four of my tires and then reopened the trunk to make sure that my spare tire was in good condition, she finally stopped her emotional but very thorough checklist. All I could say was, "Yes, Mom."

We had finally made it out of the gas station but had not made it out of the city when she started her lengthy audible intercessions and prayers. We had almost made it to the North Carolina state line, when she had finally covered my "old car," as she called it, our trip up north, her Trailways Bus trip back to Charlotte, and my four years of college in preparation for becoming a preacher, which included the money that I would need, the jobs that I would have to work, the friends that I would make and the girls that I would meet. I never did think she would stop praying over "the girls" that I would meet. We were both completely exhausted, and I hadn't said one single word in nearly two hours.

Even at the youthful age of eighteen, I clearly understood that this was an historic moment in the Kelton family. Not only would I become the first member of our family to graduate from college, but I would also become the first to enter into the ministry and become a preacher. I wanted to go to Oral Roberts University in Tulsa, Oklahoma, but realized that dream was out of reach because of the money that would be needed. I then applied at the Assemblies of God Colleges, Central Bible Institute and Evangel College, both located in Springfield, Missouri, but they were also too expensive. This venture of college was way beyond our financial means. At times we were so discouraged that we nearly gave up the dream of college.

I then discovered Mount Vernon Bible College, a small Foursquare school located in central Ohio that would not require any money up front and yet assist me in finding a job and allow me to pay them monthly. That settled the decision. Mom and I were both convinced that this was the will of God for my life and future.

Those final hours of driving were immersed in heart to heart dialogue between Mom and me. One of the subjects of conversation was in regard to my failing senior English. Mom expressed her disappointment that I was unable to walk across the platform and receive my high school diploma. I told her that it was a bitter moment that I would never forget, when I reached my hand out across the counter in the school office and received my diploma from a secretary.

With tears trickling down her cheeks, she commented about her watching me pack up all of my belongings. In reality I didn't have that much, but what really hit her emotionally was when she saw me placing my special baseball in my footlocker chest. It was special because the coach of my little league baseball team that I had been on for several years had given it to me. Coach Ken had autographed it along with all the guys on the team the summer that we moved.

She then revealed her bitter disappointment in her decision to move us from our home in Kansas City, Missouri to Charlotte, North Carolina. Our lives had been greatly impacted, both positively and negatively, by that single decision. She wondered out loud if that monumental decision had been worth leaving our home and most of our family behind. Her tearful statement to me about the reality of living in Charlotte for over six years since our arrival there along with the fact that we were now living in a third rental home seemed to be excruciating to her.

Well, back to the trip to college. When we finally arrived at the small but beautiful campus, a little over five hundred miles from Charlotte, we were both unable to talk. We looked tearfully at each other, understanding that this day would change our lives forever. We didn't know it then, but in the not too distant future, I would return to my hometown of Charlotte, and begin fulfilling the call upon my life to be a preacher. Little did we understand at that moment the roles that we each would have in each other's lives during the next four decades.

After this emotional mother helped me get settled into my dorm room on the second floor, and then after meeting Mrs. Gamble, one of my future professors; Dr. Mouer, the president of the college; and Dr. Helms, the Dean of Students, she was satisfied. We then made our way back to Columbus, about an hour's drive, and got her ready to board the Trailways Bus for her trip back to Charlotte. What I remember most about that moment was her emotional embrace. She then stuffed the last five-dollar bill that she had into my shirt pocket and climbed up the steps of the bus and tearfully said, "I'll be praying for you everyday." It was those prayers that strengthened me over the next four years of college.

My mother returned home that day knowing that she had done about all a mother could do. The rest was up to her son and his willingness to surrender to God's perfect will for his life and future. I just stood there waving at her as she tearfully waved back through the window of that noisy bus as it disappeared into the bustling traffic.

I did a lot of growing up in the next few years. Trying to discipline myself into studying in preparation for the ministry and keep my grades up in courses like "New Testament Greek," "Church History" and "Biblical Archaeology" while working forty-hour jobs to help pay the tuition fees was easier said than done. My grades were often like a roller coaster ride, and the most disappointing reality was that I made some "bad" decisions along the way.

It was a night during my sophomore year that I will never forget. I had just returned back to the campus after working an eight-hour shift in a local factory. It was after midnight and I had just made the long climb up to my fourth floor dorm room, hoping to hurry into the shower and collapse into my bed for a few hours of sleep so I could start all over the next day.

There was an unusual amount of stirring going on amongst a number of students in the dorm area. Then it happened. A number of the guys, mostly freshmen, approached me and asked if I wanted to skip out of the dorm and head into town for some pizza. I reminded them that we would be breaking the rules if we did that. The dorms were officially closed after midnight except for those of us who were working and coming in late.

To this day I still do not understand the brainless decision that the nine of us made that crucial night. Knowing that the primary entry doors were guarded by alarms, we made our way out of a window, quietly descending down the four-story fire escape. We then pushed two of our cars out of the parking lot, about the length of a football field, so as not to awaken anyone with the sound of our engines. One of those two cars was my olive green 1951 Chevrolet Coupe.

We made our way into town and devoured a half dozen or so pizzas and then hurriedly and discreetly made our way back to the campus and up that four-story fire escape. After making our way through the window, we were all smiles, thinking that we had been successful in our escapade that night. Well, one of the guys in the dorm that did not go with us had made his way to the apartment of the dorm supervisor, informing him of what we had done.

When we heard that dreadful news, most of the guys who were freshmen completely panicked. Several of them had rushed to the small lounge and fell on their knees, audibly praying. They had some mischievous and bamboozled thought that maybe they could "con" their way out of this dilemma through some sort of instant prayer vigil. All I can tell you is that I just sat down in one of the chairs in the lounge while watching and listening to those "idiots" and soberly awaited my imminent fate.

Within just a few minutes, the door opened to the lounge where all of us were huddled, with the dorm supervisor soberly making his way into the room. I shouldn't have been surprised when my eyes then fell on the sober face of the Administrative Dean, followed by the Dean of Students, followed by one of the professors that had the unenviable job as a student advisor and counselor as well. Well, as some would say in today's vernacular, "the gig was up." All of those audible prayers hoping to "con" the school authorities into thinking that these guys were a bunch of "super spiritual" students just didn't work.

It was a very dark day in my life, when I called my mother

in North Carolina from the telephone in the Dean of Student's office with the Dean of Students sitting there beside me. I had to try to explain to her what I had done and the price that I was to pay for my actions that fateful night. I had been expelled from classes for three days. I was permitted to continue to live in the dorm as well as make my way to my job, but I would not be allowed into the classroom for three days, and if I happened to miss a test or examination, too bad, I would not be able to make it up. My grade for that test missed would be a "zero."

All I can remember is the tearful and emotional one word question from my mom over that telephone line when she asked me, "Why?" None of my answers seemed to help. When we hung up, she was audibly crying.

How could I have been so stupid that miserable night? I had actually driven by that pizza parlor while on my way home from my job. I could have stopped and gone in and eaten a pizza if I was hungry, or better yet, I could have ordered those half dozen pizzas and brought them back to the dorm with me and would not have violated any rules. Then to think that I was one of the two upperclassmen that had played a significant part in this whole nightmare by packing several freshmen into my car, I was angry and disappointed with myself. Here I was hoping to become a preacher some day and influence people to do good and I am already making a stupid and ridiculous decision like this one, facilitating fellow classmates to do the same.

As the word quickly got around campus in the next day or two about our so-called "adventure" and subsequent expulsion from classes for three days, we had been tagged as "The Naughty Nine." Believe me; we were not chuckling as many of our class-mates were when they would walk by one of us.

I was thankful that our escapade that night was not any more serious than eating pizza off campus, but it did bring my thinking back to the whole reason that I was in Bible College. Just the thought of me potentially failing God after all that He had done to protect my life sobered me to a renewed commitment to the calling upon me. This was no game that I was involved in. People's eternal lives and destiny's were at stake. I was hoping that my life would someday make a difference in the lives of others.

I rarely use the word "haunt," but for many of those earlier years in my life, the fact that I did not go to Vietnam haunted me. Especially when my mind would drift back to my return home for Christmas break after only five months at college and discovered that casualties had already occurred within the Class of 1966. Yes, this was no game that I was involved in.

Only the Lord knew the sorrow that was within me as to the war in Vietnam. Every time that I would hear a current news report about the war, a sense of guilt would try to rise up within me. Many of the guys that I had graduated from high school with, the Class of 1966, were drafted. I received a 4-D classification from the local draft board permitting me to go on to Mount Vernon Bible College. One of our local officers said that upon the completion of my ministerial education, that I would possibly be positioned as a military chaplain.

Well, that flood of past emotional thoughts finally subsided. I knew without a doubt that the God of the Bible had chosen me. I didn't fully understand why he had chosen someone like me, but I was more determined than ever to not disappoint Him!

Chapter 3

A Virtuous Woman

"He who finds a wife finds a good thing,
and obtains favor from the Lord."
Proverbs 18:22

She was the cutest girl that I had ever seen. My teacher could hardly keep my attention focused toward the front of the classroom because I would just sit there and gaze at her pretty curly hair. What can you expect from a guy when you have a girl with a head of hair that beautiful sitting right in front of you every day in class. However, it was when she would turn and look at me that I would nearly lose track of what was going on in class. There was a twinkle in her eyes that captivated me.

I was determined to show her that maybe I was that special guy that she was looking for. After all, I wasn't bad looking and I was just as smart as any other guy in that classroom. Then again, things don't always work out the way you want them too.

I had been struggling with a bad cold that week and had used up all of my tissues, when I tapped her on her shoulder and asked her if I could borrow one of hers. What a miserable moment that was. She had reached for one of her tissues and had just turned around to hand it to me when I sneezed the most terrible wet and drippy sneeze that anyone could possibly carry out. I mean it was like an explosion mixed with a rainstorm all at one time.

I will never forget the look on her face when the spray from that mammoth sneeze reached her hand, arm and blouse. More menacing to my memory than the look on her face was the single word that came out of her mouth, "Yuck!" I quickly raised both of my arms in order to wipe it away on my shirtsleeves, but it was too late. The damage had been done.

My teacher had rushed to where I was sitting and quickly escorted me out of the classroom. I could hear the other students giggling as we reached the hallway. It was a day that the Antioch Kindergarten class would never let me forget.

The next morning when I arrived at school, I discovered that the curly haired, twinkle-eyed girl had asked the teacher to move her to another desk on the opposite side of the classroom. At age five, it was my first experience filled with hurt and disappointment in my search for that perfect girl in my life.

Everyone knows that by the time you make it to the fifth grade, you are pretty smart about a lot of things. You are not only good at math, but you can write very well in cursive, and if you are a guy, you certainly know how to charm the girls, especially the cute ones.

Timmy Kelton was no dummy. When Valentine's Day arrives, you make sure that the very "special" Valentine's cards get to the "special girl," or can I say girls. I was just crazy about two very cute gals named Glenda and June; however, I do admit that I was learning very early in life that it is pretty difficult to hang on to two girls at the same time.

It's not so much a problem when everyone is in the same classroom together, but the real trick is how you work it all out in the lunchroom or on the playground during recess. Of course you have your typical manly performances such as showing off the muscles in your biceps, or kicking the ball harder than anyone else, or perhaps climbing to the top of the jungle gym and balancing yourself in some kind of death defying act of bravery. That usually gets the girls' attention and admiration. However, today, on Valentine's Day, I had the perfect plan, or so I foolishly and regrettably thought.

I had looked through my pack of Valentine's cards that my mother had purchased for me and found two cards that truly expressed "love." I then signed both of them, "I Love You, Timmy K." Then after placing them in their respective envelopes, I then proudly wrote "Glenda" on one envelope and "June" on the other one.

When we were all distributing our cards to each other in class, I made sure that I had that special smile on my face when I approached each of those girls, separately, of course. I had worked out the perfect plan. I was thinking, "Timmy K., are you smart or what?"

Well, when I saw Glenda and June standing together out on the playground during recess, reading and then swapping those two Valentine's cards, I humbly realized that I had now been demoted to the "what" category. I began learning early in life that a guy was not doing very good when his girl, or I should say girls, are "glaring" at him. Suffice it to say that both Glenda and June were no longer fascinated or interested in Timmy K. Oh well, my search for that perfect girl would continue, but hopefully I would wise up along the way.

I was so grateful for the youth group that I was growing up in as a teenager. The leadership over us youth were always there for us. In spite of them being many years older than all of us teens, they seemed to always have the ability to communicate with us on our level and understand what we were facing during those critical years. Of course once in awhile they would goof up and remind us that they weren't perfect either.

I never cease to be amazed at the trouble us guys can get in to because of what many professionals describe as "male ego." I keep reminding myself over all of these years of my life that the Creator, the God of the Bible, surely was thinking something positive, beneficial and advantageous toward humankind when he designed us guys the way He did.

It was to be another one of those momentous days in the life of Tim Kelton. A lot of us teens had joined with our youth leader, Pastor Phil, for a trip to a local restaurant for fellowship and a meal together. While the original intention of such an activity was well-meaning, it turned out to be a disaster, at least for two of us.

After we had finished our main meal together, most of us then ordered some kind of a desert. Pastor Phil and I both ordered the same desert from that colorful menu that seemed to make the Banana Split that was pictured—covered with several different toppings, nuts, and a delicious looking cherry mounted on top—irresistible. Yes, it was tasting as delicious as it had been portrayed, but then it happened.

I am telling you the truth. I didn't start it. Pastor Phil started it. With his spoon, he flipped one of the little nuts covered with some whipped cream right on my shirt. He displayed his usual and unique grin as he awaited my response. You tell me please, what's a man to do in such a situation?

Well, I then flipped a peanut covered with ice cream in

return at Pastor Phil. So he quickly loaded another spoon full of sweet goodies and flipped them back at me. So, not to be denied my rightful place among the dominion of male hierarchy, I once again loaded my spoon, this time with a few more sweet and delectable ingredients, and zeroed in on his face.

He then packed his spoon full of one of everything that had come in that glass banana split bowl, and unloaded it toward me with certain fervor, but I successfully and quickly ducked beneath the table, while most of the ingredients from his spoon landed on the table directly behind me. Unfortunately, that table directly behind me had several much older patrons seated around it trying to eat their meal.

As you can only imagine, the situation was pretty dreary, especially when the manager of that Shoney's stepped up to our table, making it quite clear that both Pastor Phil and I were to "Please, leave now and do not ever come back." The only good thing that I can remember out of that entire wacky event was that I had noticed the continued embarrassed giggling of a young lady in our youth group and her twinkly eyes that had been focused upon me.

Well, I had already been eyeing this quiet-mannered and sweet-spirited young lady in our youth group named Allyson. When she would catch me looking at her, she would always respond with a gentle smile. I wasn't quite old enough to drive yet, but that didn't hinder me one Saturday, when my mother reluctantly released me to hitchhike nearly four miles to Allyson's house to spend the afternoon with her and her parents. When Mom came to pick me up that evening, my heart was throbbing with "love" for this young lady.

It was my first experience at "going steady" with a girl, and

I was crazy about her. We would get together as much as our parents would allow us. We went to the same high school and would continually look for each other at opportune times. It was also a very compelling motivation for us to make it to church and youth group meetings and youth activities every time we could. Not that we didn't love the Lord, but come on, just maybe we had each found our partner for life.

I don't really know what happened to end that relationship. I just know that when our youth group made that historic trip to David Wilkerson's Teen Challenge Center in New York City, during the summer that preceded my senior year in high school, I had come home changed. There was a determination deep inside of me to not lose sight of the calling upon my young life, and surely in God's timing, I would find the perfect lady for my life. He certainly knew that I didn't want to be alone in life or in the ministry. So what else could I do but press on?

The year was 1968. I was about to begin my junior year at Mount Vernon Bible College in Mount Vernon, Ohio, where I had been through some major struggles trying to prepare myself to become a preacher. Part of the struggle, as is with many college young people, was the issue with finances and paying the school bill. I wasn't in college on any kind of scholarship.

I had been working forty-hour jobs while taking a full load of classes. I had quit my job at Round Hill Dairy as a bottle washer. Yes, that was the day before everything went to paper cartons and plastic. I was responsible for handling thousands of those small glass school lunchroom milk bottles every week. They would come in from the local schools with dried, smelly milk all over them. Too many times, especially during the hot days, I would have to fight dozens of maggots crawling in and out of those bottles. Some nights when I would make my way back to the dorm, I would lay a bath towel in the bottom of the shower, and just sit there under the stream of water. I was hoping to drown any leftover maggots that might be hiding.

The so-called upside to that job was that I could drink all of the milk or eat all of the ice cream that I wanted. In order to keep me from resigning, the manager even released me to take treats out of the coolers at the dairy every evening for my five room-mates back at the dorm. Those five guys thought I was some kind of "miracle worker." They got so spoiled, they even started giving me their daily orders like "Just a small chocolate milk tonight, Tim," or "How about some orange juice and a half pint of ice cream." They were all pretty depressed when I resigned from the dairy and took a job as a janitor, cleaning toilets for the blue-collar workers and offices for the management at one of the major plants in town.

That job at Cooper-Bessemer was allowing me to make more money than I had ever made. I was now caught up with my school tuition and accompanying fees and was actually pay-ing money in advance and had money left over. I had never been in that position. However, it was not a pleasant job. Cleaning dozens of toilets in a grimy factory setting every day was a smelly, challenging task. Emptying a multitude of trashcans along with mopping and cleaning dirty, soiled floors every day was certainly not my life's goal.

Then another major area that I was greatly struggling with was that I had almost married the wrong girl. You would think that I would have just kept my mind on work and my studies. After all, marriage is supposed to come at a time when you are completely ready for it, right? You know, when you have all of your "ducks in row" as some say. Like a steady job or established career, with money in the bank and a house ready to move into.

I desperately wanted to find the right lady for me. I had kept praying for God's perfect will, but it seemed like nothing was ever going to work out for me. I didn't want to be in the ministry alone. In what seemed like a never-ending pursuit in my young life, I fell for Michelle, a young lady from Maine, a fellow student, and in a short period of time asked her to marry me.

We had both just finished our freshman year. She said "yes." What were we thinking, or as some of my friends said later, "not thinking?" I hadn't even met her parents in person when she purchased her wedding gown. We had set the date in spite of the college rule that stated students were not allowed to marry during their first two years of education without penalty, that penalty being that both of us would have to wait for one full semester after the marriage before we could continue on with our education toward the ministry. Both of our families had accepted our decision but expressed their concerns.

We had traveled to Charlotte in order for me to introduce her to my mother. Mom welcomed her with open arms. However, something happened during those few days. Years later, I attributed it to those mothers' prayers on that first journey to college, where she earnestly prayed that if it was God's will for this son to marry, that he would marry the right girl.

That final night in Charlotte, I stumbled with the words as I said, "Michelle, I think we are about to make a mistake. I'm not sure that we are supposed to get married." I lowered my head, feeling ashamed of myself, when she squeezed my hand and tearfully responded, "Tim, you're right." I know that it seems very strange and curious, but during that summer of 1967, we parted as friends.

The next year was very difficult for me. I actually went into a state of depression. I couldn't keep my focus on my studies. My grades were spiraling downward. Where I had been making B's and C's in my overall studies, I was now struggling to pass several classes.

I had isolated myself from most of my friends and was overwhelmed with my job. I was not doing well. When I returned home for a visit at Christmas, Mom was very worried. Even when I refused to talk with my pastor about how I was feeling, she somehow coaxed me into seeing a local counselor. I conveyed to him my disappointment in being raised without a father's influence as a young man. I also spoke of my fear that I would travel the same bitter road of anger at God mixed with booze and drugs as my older brother had lived since Dad's death. I knew that I had been called by God to preach, but I also feared being alone in that calling. I had experienced watching my mother's loneliness while raising us boys on her own, and it left its negative mark upon me. Thankfully that session did help me understand more clearly.

Not long after that trip to my home in Charlotte, I decided to make another weekend trip up north. I went alone, desiring to seek the Lord more earnestly as to my future.

I ended up at Niagara Falls, New York, my first time to see such a historic landmark in America. It was mind-boggling to read the information about how many gallons of water rushed over those rocky cliffs every single day. After several hours of walking along the walkways and gazing at the river running over the falls, a pretty bad storm moved in, accompanied by some torrential rain. So I hightailed it back to my car and decided to find me something to eat.

After chowing down several burgers, I noticed a movie theater marquee advertising its current showing. With the storm still pounding the area, and wanting to go back for one more look at Niagara Falls before I would head back toward campus, I decided to take in the movie.

Well, I would never recommend the movie *The Graduate*, starring Dustin Hoffman, but it was certainly a reality check for Tim Kelton. As I sat there watching the fictional tragedy of a young college man portrayed on that huge screen, I was sobered once again to the certainty that we become what we choose to become. As I headed back to my car at the close of the movie, I was once again renewed in my commitment to follow God's will in my life.

Thankfully, the storm had subsided, so I headed back to the falls for one final look. That moment standing at the edge of those rushing waters was to forever mark me. Some might say that I am being too melodramatic and theatrical, especially after I had just sat in a large movie theater and viewed a Hollywood movie. I can only tell you this is what I experienced.

As I stood there leaning on that aluminum guardrail, gazing into that thunderous volume of water cascading over those famous falls, the boisterous quantity of water changed into an unbelievable and very frightening image of human faces. They were young and old, male and female. They looked scared and hopeless, and there seemed to be no end to the volume of those desperate faces pouring over those cliffs.

I am not sure how long I stood there with my heart pounding within me, but I would never forget, not so much what I saw, but what I felt. For the first time in my life I sensed the reality of spiritual darkness and doom. I felt the emotion that is encased in the destiny and fate of humanity that chooses to reject God's love. It was a feeling that I never want to feel again.

I soberly made my way back to my car and tearfully headed back to the college campus in Ohio. Once again, there was a renewed determination within me to stay on course. Not one shred of doubt was within me that day, or this day, but that I had been marked to help pull some of those desperate faces out of their path to eternal destruction before my life would end.

In spite of failing several classes and actually losing a semester's credit, I struggled on in faith, believing as a young man, that God would help me find His perfect will for my future as a preacher of the Gospel. He had marked my life for His cause, and I knew it. Slowly but surely, the dark cloud lifted off of me, and there was a renewed spirit within me. This summer of 1968 now had a fresh feel to it. I was working hard on my job and had just finished making up one of my classes through a summer session. I was looking forward to my junior year in college, and I might add that I had resolved within myself that I would stay clear of the ladies on or off campus until I had finished my education, and that I had done successfully for nearly a year. Oh, I would commit to a date once in a while during what some of my friends called "a period of recovery," but I was once again a focused and determined young man.

I was standing in the cafeteria lunch line. College students are always in such a hurry because of so many goals to be accomplished during each day. I was feeling frustrated that the line was moving so slowly. Then it happened. I remember the moment like it was yesterday. She was walking out of the cafeteria after finishing her lunch. As she walked past me, she smiled at me. It was like everything came to a standstill. I returned the smile and turned not only my head, but also my whole body as she disappeared on down the hallway. She was an incoming freshman. She had beautiful, sparkling blue eyes and a smile that would stop a freight train. Similar to a famous line in a popular Hollywood movie, "She had me at the smile!"

I asked this freshman for a date, and she accepted. Claudia Sue Fannin was from New Castle, Indiana. She was just a year younger than me and had spent the previous year working while trying to save some money and make a decision about college. With a profound experience with Christ, she had made her way to this same small Bible College in Ohio to determine the will of God for her life and future.

After many deep conversations about God's calling upon each of our lives, and our future expectations for ministry and considering our family back grounds, including the sobering fact that I had nearly married someone else, we discerned that God had brought us together. I proposed marriage to Claudia on New Years Eve, 1968. Our three children, who are all grown now, still rib me about such a short period of time between our first meeting standing in that college cafeteria hallway and a marriage proposal on the following New Years Eve.

Claudia's mom and dad were skeptical, and rightly so. They had sent their only daughter off to college, and in less than six months she was talking marriage. Claude and Mary Fannin were hard working, small-town people. My first meeting with them was when they, along with Claudia's only sibling, Larry, traveled to the college campus to get a look at this guy that she had been telling them about. It was definitely my mistake when I treated her family to a Mexican Restaurant located several miles off campus. Claudia's dad was not to keen on tacos. He definitely was a burger kind of guy. Oh well, you live and learn.

Claudia and I had decided to set the date for marriage in the summer of 1969. We were deeply in love and didn't see why we should wait any longer. We also knew in our hearts that no further decisions should be made unless we had the blessing of our parents. So the first step was that I would travel alone to spend the weekend with Claudia's mom and dad. They both inherently knew why I had come.

It was Saturday night. Claudia's dad and I were sitting on their small front porch. He was sitting in a rocker-type chair and I was securely planted on a small swing chair. I was usually susceptible to motion sickness, but couldn't tell whether my inner sickness was a result of the motion on that swing chair or the emotion of that historic moment.

"Tim, you can do this," I kept telling myself. "All you have to do is tell Mr. Fannin that you love his daughter and you want to marry her and that you would like his approval and blessing."

Her dad and I were both worn out from rocking. It was getting late. The sun had set hours ago. Then finally, we had a breakthrough. Claudia's mom opened the screen door, glaring at both of us and sparked, "Will you please ask Claude for permission to marry Claudia, so we can go to bed!"

Claudia's dad and I both stopped our motions in those chairs immediately. We momentarily looked at each other nervously. I sucked in some air and looked at him squarely in the face. I simply said, "Mr. Fannin, I would like your permission to marry Claudia." His simple but forthright reply was, "Do you love my daughter?"

Today, after many years myself as a father, I've learned that it's not easy to give a daughter to another man. A daughter that you have loved and nurtured since birth and have worked long and tedious hours to provide for. A daughter that you would have given your life to protect from harm. I admit that my response was nervous while I was looking into those father's eyes, but it was genuine. I said, "Yes sir, I love your daughter, and always will!"

Claudia and I then traveled to North Carolina in order to introduce her to my mother. From their very first meeting, Mom loved and accepted Claudia. There seemed to be a certain peace exhibited within my mother not only about Claudia, but also our decision to get married. After all, she had been praying for at least three years that this son would find the right girl.

As Mr. Fannin escorted Claudia down the aisle of her home church in that beautiful wedding gown, with no visible smile upon his face, you would have thought that maybe this was a funeral instead of a wedding. However, he admitted to me years later that he was very nervous about Claudia marrying a preacher, and in his own way asked me to forgive him for his frown on that eventful day. He stood firm in support of us as a couple. Claude Fannin became a father to me.

At the end of that historic wedding day, Saturday, July 26, 1969, we headed back towards the campus and our small three-room apartment. We spent our wedding night in a Howard Johnson's Motel somewhere along Interstate 70. We made it back in time for both Claudia and I to be on our jobs on Monday. That's certainly not how I would recommend any newlywed couple to begin their married life, but that's how it was for us.

A year later, after graduation from college and before we would move to our first pastoral assignment, I asked Claudia if she would like to travel to Niagara Falls with me. Because of our job schedules, we would only have one full day at the falls.

It is still a very pleasant memory of Claudia and I lying together on our huge blanket sprawled out on the grassy area adjacent to the thunderous waterfalls. We had just finished devouring an entire watermelon, one of Claudia's favorite fruits, when I rehearsed to her my earlier visit and subsequent experience standing at the waters edge of Niagara Falls. Of course, she had previously heard my story, but at that precise moment, sitting close to those extraordinary falls, it seemed more real. It comforted and inspired me all the more, now that I had someone special to join with me in this determined effort to *change the world*.

Chapter 4

GOD IS FAITHFUL; YOU BE FAITHFUL

"For we do not wrestle against flesh and blood,
but against principalities,
against powers, against the rulers of the darkness of this age,
against spiritual hosts of wickedness in the heavenly places."
Ephesians 6:12

Tim and Claudia Kelton were happy to be married, but like so many newlyweds, we were rapidly discovering that married life is not all "ecstasy, harmony, and wedded bliss." We were both working fulltime jobs. I had just taken a new job at the General Motors parts plant in Mansfield, Ohio, and was carpooling to work each day the challenging distance of seventy miles along with four other college friends. I was trying to prepare myself for my senior year in college. As a couple, we were trying to prepare ourselves for future ministry. This is not the kind of scenario that I would recommend for any young married couple.

One of the most sorrowful memories of those early months of our marriage came as a result of Claudia and I becoming so agitated with each other over the frustrations with our work and class schedules, accompanied by the lack of maturity as a married couple, that we found ourselves in the midst of a meltdown. It was a sad but eye-opening moment.

Our small bathroom had been constructed in what had been

a walk-in closet, and it was the only door that we had on the inside of our apartment. The sink was directly at the center of the closet. We could not even brush our teeth in privacy because there was barely enough space for the closet door to close. When we needed to shower, we would have to suck in oxygen and press through to the left. When we needed to use the toilet, we would have to suck in air and press through to the right. Now, if you are wondering where I am going with all of these details, let me explain a little further.

Somewhere in our lives we had been mesmerized into thinking that when you are upset with your mate, a good way to demonstrate your frustration and place an exclamation mark at the point of your frustration, was to "slam a door" in their face! That will show them!

Of course, to accomplish that scenario in our small apartment was not easy. First of all, you had to be quick enough to reach the door before the other one could. You then had to quickly suck in air and, like lightening, maneuver your way to the left or right and into the bathroom. It would almost take a miracle for all of that to happen. Well, one day a miraculous event did occur.

At one eventful moment, we were both so frustrated and annoyed with each other over something—we don't even remember what it was—that at break neck speed we arrived at that crazy bathroom doorknob at the same time. Something remarkable happened when our hands touched each other. We were both embarrassed at our actions and were instantly reminded that we were a young married couple that actually loved each other. Why on earth had we been behaving like such idiots? Tears welled up in both of our eyes as we hugged each other and made a commitment that day that we would never be so foolish again. That was not to say that our marriage relationship would never face another challenge, but we were more committed than ever that we would be more sensitive to each other's needs. Well, in short order, we would be tested once again.

Our small three-room apartment was only a few blocks from the campus, which made it nice for me trying to get to classes under the extreme pressure that I was feeling as to my daily schedule. Our apartment was one of four small apartments situated within a large two-story house. Unfortunately, while the outward condition of that old house was cosmetically pleasant to the eyes, it was physically and structurally in pretty bad shape.

We had readily noticed that the distance between the baseboards around our small rooms were gradually increasing from the floors. In other words, the floors were sagging and separating from the walls. Yes it made us nervous, but we just needed to make it through only one year, then we would be out of there, right?

Well, we were both getting pretty jumpy when we started seeing a number of varieties of insects making their way into our apartment, especially the night we rolled back the blanket on our mattress in order to go to bed and then eye-balled a huge, furry, long legged, fast moving spider make his way toward where we were standing. All I can tell you is that spider single-handedly snatched away the romantic mood that we were both in. On my inspection of our little apartment the next day, I was able to see daylight, and that was not just through our windows.

Not too many nights from that night, I finally made it home after an exhausting day of four separate one-hour classes, eight hours of strenuous work in a plant and a seventy-mile road trip to find my bride standing on top of my footlocker chest. After entering through the door, I was stunned to see her tearfully and fretfully, with hands cupped together, just standing there staring down at the floor. It took me a few seconds to zero in on our newest invading predator that had entered the apartment, and when I did, unfortunately, I made one of my first major errors that a young, newlywed husband could make, I chuckled. I reached down with one of my hands and slowly picked up from the carpet, a small baby frog.

Claudia didn't speak to me for a while that evening, but I clearly understood that as I had exited the back door to take the little frog outside, that we were going to start looking for another place to live and that I would need to humbly apologize for my silly grin and insensitive chuckle.

To this day, thirty-seven years later, I still don't know how long my special lady had been standing on that footlocker chest before I came home and rescued her. Oh well, it doesn't really matter. A few weeks later, after a very serious event with the smell of gas in the apartment, and subsequent discovery of a major weakness in the natural gas lines within the whole structure by the local fire department, we finally moved to another apartment in the heart of town.

Still excited about entering into the ministry, we had communicated with Dr. Teffeteller, the supervisor of the Southeast District of our Foursquare denomination. We had expressed our desire to pastor in the city of Charlotte, but he told us that there was only one Foursquare Church in the city and a recent graduate from our college was pastoring it.

Claudia and I then decided that we would communicate with Garr Memorial Church, located in the city of Charlotte, and see if there might be an opening for us in my home church. However, while the pastors communicated that there was no opening for us, they heartily invited us to the city and the church.

Dr. Teffeteller then phoned us and asked us to consider a pastoral assignment in the state of Mississippi. It was an established church that would welcome a new young couple as their pastors. Well, after a lot of prayer and consideration, we sensed that God had called us to the city of Charlotte, and decided that we would move there, find us a place to live, each get a job, and then join the recent graduates from our college and help them in any way that we could.

It was after our call to that young couple advising them of our decision, hoping that they would find it acceptable, that they then related to us that after only one year in Charlotte, they were in the process of tendering their resignation to Dr. Teffeteller's office and would be seeking a new assignment. We were stunned and thrilled at the same time. Dr. Teffeteller made the official decision for us to become the new pastors in Charlotte. All we had to do was make it through school and graduate.

We were deeply saddened to discover over the next few months that the young couple in Charlotte had vacated their position earlier than expected with some kind of conflict with the membership within the small congregation. The church had actually closed as a result.

Dr. Teffeteller had made his way from North Carolina to the graduation ceremonies in Mount Vernon, Ohio. It was during that historic time that he pulled us aside and communicated to us his deep disappointment as to the seven-year effort of trying to establish a Foursquare Church within the city of Charlotte. He recounted the six pastoral appointments since the church's inception in 1963, and the investment in prayer, effort and finances that had only ended with another disappointing conclusion. He showed his frustration and sorrow.

I remember it like it was yesterday, when he gently but sternly looked us in the eyes and stated, "We are appointing you all as the seventh pastors in seven years to the Foursquare Church in Charlotte." He continued, "You will receive no financial funding from my office or the denomination. You will have to take care of yourselves." He then concluded with, "If it is God's will for you two to establish a Foursquare church in the city of Charlotte, then let it be so! You will have my prayers, but if this fails again, then we will close the church permanently!"

He admitted to us that the continued failure to plant a church in the city of Charlotte baffled him. Dr. Teffeteller reviewed with us the reality of prospering, healthy Foursquare churches that had been established over many years in numerous towns and cities that encircled the city of Charlotte, but nothing seemed to work for the denomination within this growing city.

While disappointed with the most recent news pertaining to the church being closed before our arrival, and the very sobering review of negative results for our denomination over the years, we were determined to press on. We both knew that God had called us at such a time as this, and we were learning early, that with the God of the Bible, *timing is everything*. Thankfully graduation was now complete. With Claudia's parents and our good friend Gary Fairchild, helping us load up our belongings in our two vehicles, and an EZ-Haul truck, we then made the move to Charlotte. This would be a move that would forever mark our lives.

We were so excited about our first pastorate. It was the summer of 1970. It just didn't seem to bother us that we had been appointed as pastors over a church that had been closed for several months. It was painfully true that the people who would be considered as members had actually withdrawn. The church building itself was a partially renovated old farmhouse on the outskirts of this bustling city of Charlotte, North Carolina.

Obviously, because there were no current members, there was no money for any pastoral income. So both Claudia and I heartily took outside jobs in the city in order to take care of ourselves. We were very grateful that our denomination had purchased a beautiful brick home adjacent to that old white farmhouse church building. We rolled up our sleeves, so to speak, and energetically began our labors for the Lord. We had looked over what few church records that we could find, hoping to find names of at least some of the past members. We wanted to visit each one that we could find and invite them to church. However, we also recognized that the building and grounds were not very inviting. So, after we started getting some paychecks from our jobs, we began making changes.

The first thing that we did was to repair and repaint the broken down sign located in front of the church. We then tackled the tall weeds and grass. My brother David, who was helping us mow the grass on his riding mower, would sometimes disappear in the tall grass. Then we struggled trying to get the old well working, and when we were finally successful with getting the water rolling through the pipes, we were frantically trying to shut the well back down because of all of the water that was pouring from the walls and through the ceilings. The next big challenge was buying many gallons of barn-red paint and then painting the entire exterior of the church. We were really excited when that huge dump truck dropped a load of gravel close to our main entrance. We actually had a visible parking area now.

Well, the neighbors took notice immediately. One neighbor actually expressed to us that he had wondered if the "Foursquare Church was in some way connected to the U-Haul Company." He told us that he knew something was different about us, because we pulled up in an EZ-Haul truck. Claudia and I just grinned at him. A number of our neighbors became very cordial toward us just for the positive transformation that was taking place. The property was not such an "eyesore" anymore. We were so excited in how God was blessing our efforts. In less than one year, we had twenty-five members in attendance at the First Foursquare Gospel Church, better known in the community as "The Little Red Church."

Claudia and I were slowly coming to grips with the realization that pastoring was much more than a building and grounds. Oh, we knew that in our hearts, but found ourselves caught in that very common dilemma of being acceptable to society, our families, our friends and to our God, the God of the Bible. The term you hear pretty often today is "being politically correct." Well, our very first test of allegiance was upon us.

God was bringing strong conviction upon my young heart as to the traditional celebration in America pertaining to Halloween. On our first Halloween in this our first pastorate, I had dressed up in a black cape, much like you would commonly see a magician dressed in. Add to that a special black hat that I wore and then that special gel that I had purchased in order to make "magical smoke" appear from my fingers, which pleasantly surprised and seemed to please our small group of members and their children.

After all, my saintly mother had hosted many Halloween parties at our home, with all the ghostly trimmings. It was no wonder that I then quickly took on the task of helping to spear-

78

head a "haunted house" party on the campus of the Foursquare Bible College that I had spent four years preparing for the ministry at. In important places that I had grown up in, there seemed to be no conviction or concern of any negative consequences, spiritually, as to Halloween. Well, deep, heartfelt conviction had come upon my heart. As a result, I would never be the same.

I had been teaching from my pulpit about the convictions that I was feeling towards Halloween as well as some other areas that were concerning me. I readily admit that in my youthfulness, I had not matured into an eloquent preacher and was "hammering" the members pretty hard. So hard, it brought us to a showdown.

The handful of men that I had as members confronted me with the demand that I stop preaching and teaching with such negative tones. We dialogued extensively, to only inflame the situation all the more. Then came the demand, "We do not want to hear the words 'devil' or 'demon' mentioned again in your sermons or we will all leave!" I was completely devastated and heartbroken to tears.

It was now Saturday night, and I had been laboring over what to preach on Sunday morning. I had been writing down some thoughts and researching Scriptures relating to "God's love," a sermon that no one could object to. The problem that was hampering me was that I just couldn't seem to concentrate or think clearly. In fact, the more I wrestled with trying to think through my sermon for that next day so that I would clearly stay away from the subject of the "devil," I began to notice that I was experiencing a difficult time in breathing.

As I kept thinking about how late it was and that I was just worn out, it then hit me like a ton of bricks. "Tim Kelton, what are you doing?" I thought. "You can't preach the truth in your sermons and never mention the 'devil'!"

I then felt the heat of conviction run through me. I stood up from behind my small desk in that humble office and raised both of my arms toward heaven, asking God to forgive me for even thinking about such a compromise. I sat back down, weeping over how easily I had been duped and deceived. This Saturday night was to change my life dramatically, forever.

As I sat at my desk rewriting my sermon notes on into the night, with a new message now burning within me—*The Temptations of Christ*—the door to my office that had been half open slammed shut. I literally jumped out of my chair. My heart skipped several beats. I hurried to the door to see who had entered our small sanctuary just outside of my office. I saw no one. After I regained my composure, I finished my sermon preparation and headed back to the parsonage located next door. I was exhausted, but at peace with God.

Sunday morning had arrived on schedule. I entered our sanctuary with that same peace that I had closed out Saturday night with. All of our families were present. Everyone seemed in good spirits. After we sang a number of hymns and choruses in worship, I then stepped up to that humble wooden pulpit. I opened my Bible to the Gospels, and in as non-threatening a manner as I could, briefly expressed that my desire as a pastor was to teach the Truth as I began my message on *The Temptations of Christ*. Our hearts were broken when most of those families chose to never return after that Sunday morning.

One older couple that had decided to remain a part of our church extended an invitation to Claudia and I to visit them at their home. As we sat together at their kitchen table enjoying some of her fresh baked apple pie, Edith soberly began her description of her recent dream.

"Pastor Tim, Marvin and I were in bed asleep last Saturday night, when all of a sudden I saw you sitting at your office desk. Your head was down, and you looked as though you were very troubled." She continued, "You also appeared to be laboring in order to breathe. It was then that my dream turned into a nightmare. I saw this huge, long snake spread out across your small bookshelves behind you. I started screaming at you to run, but you made no move. The snake then slithered off of your shelves and onto your desk and began to wrap itself around you, squeezing you more tightly every moment, with its fangs and forked tongue glaring at you, right in your face. I kept screaming at you and wondering at the same time why you did nothing to escape the snake. Then all of a sudden, you stood to your feet lifting your hands toward the ceiling and began weeping. The large snake fell to the floor and slithered its way out of your office. Pastor, that snake was angry when it flipped its tail to slam your office door shut. I then woke up. I was so startled at what I saw; I also awakened Marvin. We laid there for hours praying for you and Claudia."

Claudia and I were completely stunned. What Edith described in her dream provided a clear and sober understanding to what I had experienced on that historic Saturday night. I then laid my head on their kitchen table and began weeping again, but these tears were tears of joy and thankfulness to the awesome God of the Bible who was watching over a *nobody* like me.

We were making every effort to overcome the deep hurt and sorrow that lingered in our hearts from the split in our small congregation. This was a very difficult time for us. We had lost people that we had learned to deeply love and care for. However, this major event in our lives was challenging us to think outside of the four walls of our small church building in order to see new members added to our congregation.

We had printed a one-page hand out telling about our church, our beliefs as well as our location. We would walk through the surrounding neighborhoods and place the fliers in people's doors. Sometimes we were blessed with the opportunity to dialogue with interested folks.

We had even asked permission from a contractor who was building a number of new homes across the street from our church property if we could walk inside the structures and pray over them. He was a little taken back with our request, but still gave us his approval. Claudia and I would usually stand in what was to be a living room, hold hands and pray that God's blessing would rest upon that residence and that He would give us the opportunity to minister to the family that would someday move in. Over the next few years, we would see results from each of those efforts to reach out to our community. However, we were gradually being impassioned for the whole city of Charlotte.

I felt deeply that God had given me another idea for reaching out to the larger city, in spite of being situated on the outskirts of the city. I had read about a motion picture that was showing on the west coast, *The Cross and the Switchblade*. It caught my attention because of not only having read the book by the same title, but that I had preached my first sermon on the streets of Harlem, in New York City, where David Wilkerson had touched so many lives through his powerful ministry called Teen Challenge Center. The movie was starring Pat Boone as David Wilkerson and Erik Estrada as the violent gangster named Nicky Cruz.

I had set up an appointment with the owner of the Carolina Theater, located in the heart of downtown Charlotte. Upon entering his office, I asked him to consider showing the movie at his theater. He asked, "What's the catch?" I replied, "I will help promote the movie through the local churches and surrounding towns." "What's the catch?" he replied once again.

I nervously responded, "Well, if you would allow me to bring my small church family and position ourselves in the mezzanine, we would be able to talk to interested viewers after each showing of the movie." The owner then nervously asked, "And how would the viewers know that you and your members were up in the mezzanine?"

By this time my voice was nearly a whisper from the intensity of the moment, saying, "I thought that maybe, perhaps, uh, I could speak over your public address system at the end of each showing, and invite interested people to the mezzanine." He then quickly stood up from behind his desk and glaringly spouted, "There will be no altar call given at the Carolina Theater!"

Before I could respond, he walked over to the door of his office, opening it, telling me that he was not interested. All the way back home, I cried while I shouted audibly to myself, "Tim Kelton, you are such an idiot! You didn't say one thing correctly! You looked and acted like a complete fool!"

I walked in the door of our home wondering what I was going to say to Claudia. To my surprise, she was waiting at the door saying, "Honey, the owner of the Carolina Theater just called and wants you to come back to his office, so you can go over the details of showing the movie." I just stopped in my tracks. My mouth was wide open in disbelief. I kissed Claudia and hurried back to downtown Charlotte.

Here are just a few of the details. Our church had distributed several hundred special fliers through the mail to churches of all denominations within the city of Charlotte as well as churches in the numerous surrounding towns and cities. He made it clear that our church would receive no money as a result of this endeavor. I agreed. He made me promise that I would not mention Jesus, God or the name of my church, but that he would allow me to speak over his public address system and briefly invite any interested persons to the mezzanine for further discussion about what they had just seen on the movie. I was pleasantly surprised and deeply grateful for this opportunity and quickly agreed. He then stated that he would continue to sell all of his snacks and soft drinks at the concession bar as usual. I agreed.

In spite of it being cold and rainy during that second week in December, over 2,000 tickets were sold. Our handful of members were thrilled at the response. They had compared their work and family schedules with each other in order to make sure that a few of them would be at each showing of the movie. Claudia and I had done the same with our schedules.

As we were approaching the final day of showing the movie, the owner pulled me aside and then asked me if I would like to continue for one additional week. He was radiating a joyful smile and friendly demeanor. Completely stunned, I agreed. The second week drew more than 3,000 additional patrons. In the end, forty-eight people made their way to the mezzanine.

One local gang member gave me his knife and accepted Christ. With tears running down his cheeks, this young man was visibly shaken by the message of that movie. He worshipped with us at our church for a few weeks but was struggling with this "all white" congregation. I was able to introduce him to another pastor and church family in which God profoundly raised him up in the coming years as one of their youth leaders. I have kept that knife all of these years as a reminder to me of God's awesome grace and compassion.

A prostitute who was deeply depressed and suicidal was set free from her life of despair. She openly wept as our ladies gathered around her in earnest and sincere prayer over her life. She told us that she had only come into the afternoon matinee in order to take a few hours of refuge from the cold, rainy weather.

A youth leader that came with his large youth group was all smiles when he shook my hand while thanking me for making this whole event possible. I was quick to tell him that the Lord was truly the One that had made it all possible. Not one of those people became a part of our congregation, but we knew that we had sown good seed into many lives that would some day come back to us.

At the end, the owner invited me back into his office. It was an awkward moment for me. It's hard to explain, but I knew that this man was not the same man that I had met just a few weeks earlier. My sense was that he had been devoted to God earlier in his life and these past two weeks had stirred his heart once again.

After we were both seated, he gently reached over his desk, handing me an envelope. I just looked at the envelope and then back at him as he gently said, "Open it."

I nervously opened that envelope and then tearfully said, "Thank you, sir." It was a check written out to our church in the amount of $500, earmarked "Building Fund." Little did any of us know or discern at that historic moment that three years from that very month of December, we would dedicate our new, four hundred-seat sanctuary.

Chapter 5

FILLED TO OVERFLOW

"It is more blessed to give than to receive."
Acts 20:35

I was riding on a high. The success of the movie The Cross and the Switchblade at the Carolina Theater in downtown Charlotte, North Carolina, was still fresh in my heart.

I was driving to the other side of the city of Charlotte, asking for another successful endeavor. I had contacted the local Rescue Mission, asking for their help in locating a family that we as a small church could bless during this Christmas season. They had given me the names of an elderly couple, Isaac and Martha Green. According to the information given me, they were a couple in great need of assistance.

They lived off of the main highway in a remote location. As I walked down the overgrown and muddy driveway, my eyes fell upon a small, rundown house. As I knocked on the plain wooden door, I had no idea how much my life and that of my small church family was getting ready to be changed.

A silver haired, wrinkle-faced lady just barely opened the door. I introduced myself and asked if I could come in and talk to her and her husband. She timidly stepped out on to the small squeaky porch pulling the door closed behind her.

"Ma'am, my church would like to bless you and your husband with some special gifts for Christmas." She just stared at me. I continued, "We would like to come back in a few days with those gifts, if that's okay with you folks?" She turned toward the door, sticking her head inside and said, "Isaac, come out here."

As a small elderly man with a cane stepped outside, she quickly repeated my words to him. He dropped his cane. It bounced off of the porch. He then lifted both feeble arms toward Heaven, "Thank you, Lord!" was his continued statement.

My eyes switched back to her. She was standing with her chin against her chest, while tears were dropping on the wooden planks. He then reached out and took my hand and began praying a blessing upon my life. As I drove back home, there was a definite sense that I would never forget this particular day or this unique and extraordinary couple.

In a few days, we returned. After sharing my experience of that day with the members of our church, they doubled and tripled everything that they had originally planned to give. We walked in with a roasted turkey and all of the trimmings. Several homemade pies along with grocery bags full of canned fruit and vegetables as well as several wrapped gifts. We had soon overloaded their small kitchen table, and we were all smiles.

One of the men motioned for me to look at their small refrigerator. I opened the door to discover that it was not only empty, but radiated no coolness. We discovered that it hadn't worked for several months. Then we were all shaken when it was apparent that they had no running water. They had been carrying water in plastic jugs from the Texaco gas station near the street entrance to their driveway. The sympathetic manager had been allowing them to use the restrooms as well. Over the next few days we were able to repair their refrigerator, get the well working and the water flowing once again. We were one exhausted but smiling church family.

They were so excited as I was helping them get into my car for Sunday's worship service. They both chuckled and praised God all the way to our humble church building located on the outskirts of the city. Upon arrival, they marched to the front row of our little fifty-seat sanctuary. Both of their voices could be heard above the rest of us as we sang several hymns and choruses. I don't think I have ever received so many "Amens!" during any sermon while I have been in the ministry as I did during that single Sunday morning.

Our entire church family was quite excited when we learned that, while Mr. Green was unable to read or write, he could actually read his Bible. He came from a very sad family background and had only attended school for a few years in his early childhood. Mrs. Green told me that he could only sign his monthly Social Security check with an "X." I just had a hard time believing it and tested him a couple of times. I asked him to read the headlines to the Charlotte Observer newspaper to me, and after looking at the front page of the paper for several minutes, he simply said, "Preacher, I can't."

I then placed one of my Bible reference books in front of him and asked him to read to me. Again, after a few minutes gently looking and turning several of the pages, he softly responded, "Preacher, I can't read anything but the Bible."

I then handed him my Bible and asked him to open it and read to me. "Preacher, what do you want me to read" he asked? I responded with, "Wherever you want, Mr. Green." He then opened my Bible to Genesis and read, and then turned to Isaiah, then Jeremiah, and then he turned to the New Testament and read what he called his favorites, the Gospels. I did finally believe this miracle.

Several months had gone by when Mrs. Green asked me to pray with her. "Preacher, you and your church family have been faithfully driving to our home to bring us to church every Sunday. I want you to pray that God would help me get my driver's license back."

I just stared at her. I know my mouth must have dropped open because she commented about it as she repeated her request. Well, I took her hands in mine and prayed. In all honesty, it was the most pathetic, faithless prayer that I had ever prayed. She clapped her hands together when I said "Amen." She then said, "Now pray that God will help us get a car."

I didn't think that it would be possible for any pastor to pray two consecutive, worthless and faithless prayers in a row. She clapped her hands together again when she heard my "Amen," and then said, "You watch, preacher! God answers prayer!" My thought inwardly was, "Not those two prayers, Mrs. Green."

Claudia asked me later, "Honey, what was that all about with Mrs. Green?" My final response was, "Claudia, there is no way on God's green earth that the state of North Carolina will give Mrs. Green a driver's license."

A few weeks later, the doorbell rang at the parsonage early Saturday morning. I stumbled to the door to be greeted by Mrs. Green. She excitedly said, "Preacher, will you please come out and baptize our new car!" I stood there in total disbelief, staring at that used, white Chevrolet station wagon, with Mr. Green and his cane standing tearfully by the hood. Mrs. Green was tearfully waving her new driver's license in the air while she was praising God for answering her pastor's prayers. I could also hear her joyfully saying, "Thank God, we can bring our grandkids to church now."

Mrs. Green then handed me her new North Carolina driver's license. Yes, it was legal. Her name was on it. It noted two restrictions. She must wear her glasses while driving, and she could only drive during daylight hours. I was once again stunned beyond belief. Then she tearfully hugged me while saying, "Preacher, you sure do know how to pray!"

Mr. Green was now dragging my garden hose from the back of the parsonage, while tearfully asking me to go ahead and baptize their car. Well, I had baptized people but had no clue how you baptize a car. I had never been so speechless in my young life. I didn't even dare consider the theology of this moment, and was hoping that no spiritual authority over me would find out what I was about to do.

I turned the outside faucet on for the garden hose while looking nervously to see if any of our neighbors were watching. I then raised the hose with a blast of water across their car saying, "In the name of the Father," followed by another blast of water across the car saying, "In the name of the Son," and yet another blast of water, "In the name of the Spirit."

Mr. Green was wiping away his tears with a handkerchief, and Mrs. Green was clapping her hands in joyful praise to her Lord, who had answered their prayers. Their pastor was—well, in all truthfulness, words cannot express.

The next day, which was Sunday morning, after driving themselves to church with one of their grandchildren, Mr. and Mrs. Green were all smiles. After the service was completed, she walked over to me and tenderly placed something in the palm of my hand as we greeted each other. I looked to see that it was a five-dollar bill.

I immediately responded, "Mrs. Green, I can't take this money. I know how you and Mr. Green struggle financially." I was sobered as my eyes fell on her wounded facial expression as she then responded, "Do you mean that if God spoke to my heart to give my pastor a gift, that my gift doesn't matter?"

I humbly and sincerely apologized to her and then thanked her for her gift as I placed that five-dollar bill in my shirt pocket. Yes, "It is more blessed to give than to receive."

I kept that precious gift for several months, wondering how I should spend it. I then put it towards a special Bible study and reference book that I needed.

In those earlier years of our pastoring, my wife and I both had to work outside jobs. Claudia was working as a bookkeeper for a major firm that supplied thread to numerous North and South Carolina mills. I had just resigned from my job as a shipping clerk for a school supply company, because they were requiring me to work half of a day on Saturday. After putting in forty hours Monday through Friday, we desperately needed the weekends free in order to concentrate on the church.

Being unsuccessful in job-hunting on my own, I tried an employment agency. They connected me to the Stewart Sand-wich Company, located near the Charlotte Airport, on the opposite side of the city from where we lived. They hired me almost immediately. I would need to be on the job at 7 a.m. every weekday morning. I was going to be responsible for delivering a variety of sandwiches to all of the 7–11 convenience stores within the metropolitan area of the city. My workday would be about nine hours.

The Stewart Sandwich Company produced a very popular menu of sandwiches that could be heated in their special ranges, on site, at each convenience store location. I was surprised at the amount of sales of these sandwiches. It was nothing for me to carry in an armload of cartons, each filled with a dozen of these individually wrapped sandwiches, two to three times weekly to the individual stores.

My on-the-job training started almost immediately with a supervisor who was assigned to me for two weeks. From the first day of training, that supervisor communicated with me about his wife, who was very sick and in the hospital. She had been diagnosed with a life-threatening disease. Ron was not a Christian, but because of the dilemma that he was in, his heart was very open. I had been introduced to all of the men at the company as the first preacher that they had ever hired. Each of their faces expressed nervousness when they shook my hand. However, each one of them verbally expressed their hope that I would be able to encourage Ron during my brief time of training with him.

Before those two weeks of training were completed, a great crisis was upon us. I remember it like it happened yesterday. We were at a 7–11 on the outskirts of Charlotte, when Ron was called to the store telephone. It seemed like everything just stopped. He slowly hung up the phone and just stood staring at the floor. I set down the cartons of sandwiches that I was working in the cooler and quickly walked to where he was standing. "Ron, is everything okay," I asked?

He then turned toward me, putting his face on my shoulder and began to weep. "She just died, Tim. My wife, she's dead."

It was my first funeral as a pastor. The company closed down for that day with all of the managers and employees in attendance. I will never forget the image of that small daughter sitting on her dad's lap, both of them weeping, and his fellow employees gathered around them with their heads bowed.

The respect that I gained from that single event was startling. Ron and his daughter began attending our small church, along with several other families from the company. I was spending a little more time each day at the warehouse, counseling and talking with many of the other employees. I was touching on everything from marital problems to financial woes.

In fact, I had now been asked to pray over the meal at the annual Christmas party where all of the employees and their mates were in attendance. I was to find out later that this particular Christmas party was a bust as a result of Claudia and I, and my prayer that included not only the meal but their individual lives, marriages, families, relationships and finances.

"Tim, the hotel lost money on the lack of alcohol consumed because of the way you prayed over all of us," confided Ron, who was grinning sheepishly.

Well, a new challenge was just around the corner for me. The top manager made his way to my truck, where I was busy loading it for that days deliveries.

"Tim, I need to talk with you about some changes on your particular route." With that, we headed to his office as he explained that they wanted me to cover a number of "bars and lounges" throughout the city, all new accounts.

"We have taken into consideration that you are a pastor, and have set up the schedule for the first thing in the mornings before they open for business," he stated. "The only one that may trouble you is a 'topless lounge' across town, but you are the only one that we trust to service it. If you know what I mean." He softly continued, "Tim, we've worked it out with the 'topless lounge' for you to meet the owner there hours before the girls show up. We really need your help here. You've been an excellent employee, and this change will come with a good raise on your paycheck. We know you can use the increase in money. Okay?" He then reached his hand out to shake my hand while glowing with a smile. "Okay," I nervously responded, sticking my hand toward him like an immature kid who couldn't find the word "No."

That evening when I tried to explain to Claudia about the decision to service numerous bars and a "topless lounge" that I had agreed to, she just stared—no, I think it was glared—at me. That was our first deep conversation with no words spoken, as a fairly new married couple.

The next morning, I nervously walked in the first bar with an armload of sandwiches and began that day's ordeal of servicing these new customers. I then made my way to the next bar, and then ... the "topless lounge." The parking lot looked empty as I drove my truck round the side of the building to the rear door. There was a single car parked close to the door. Nervous is not an accurate word as to my demeanor. Panic would be more accurate.

With an armful of cartons of sandwiches, a mouth dry as a bone and a heart pounding in my chest, I knocked on the door. The door popped open almost immediately. "Hey, Al, it's the sandwich man you're waiting on," she shouted!

There I stood with my mouth wide-open. I'm pretty sure that my heart actually stopped. I couldn't get air in my lungs. She was bubbly, all smiles, and naked, except for the G-string around her waist. "Follow me," she motioned.

I stumbled twice as we made our way through the dimly lit corridor to the back of the bar where the refrigerator was located. She bent over and opened the refrigerator door, pointing at a couple of empty racks for the sandwiches.

As I was speedily stuffing the cartons in, she said, "So, you're a preacher, huh?" In all truthfulness, I nearly fell into the refrigerator myself. "Where's your church," she asked?

I stood up, closing the door to the fridge with a frenzied motion for the owner, who was standing behind her, to sign my delivery receipt. "Excuse me, ma'am," I said as I swiftly made my way around her, back down the corridor to the door. My knees were so weak that I wasn't sure that I would make it back to the truck. All I was thinking about was the potential headlines in the Charlotte Observer newspaper the next day, "Preacher Caught At Local Topless Lounge."

"Hey, mister," she shouted while waving at the door, "You forgot your receipt!" My mind was numb as I just looked at her while trying to back the truck up so I could escape.

"Hey! Hey! Stop," she motioned! I stopped and rolled the window further down so I could hear what she was trying to say. "What's your favorite sandwich," she questioned? I just looked at her and mumbled in total disbelief, "Ham n' cheese, ma'am, ham n' cheese."

That was the first and last "topless lounge" that I ever visited. I turned in my two weeks notice that afternoon.

Chapter 6

HAVE FAITH IN GOD

"For as the heavens are higher than the earth,
so are My ways higher than your ways,
and My thoughts than your thoughts."
Psalm 126:5

I was so excited about this day that was before me. I had just kissed Claudia, saying, "Honey, today I finally feel like a successful pastor. This is a Sunday that we'll always remember." I then hurried out the door to go join Fred for our very first bus run. It was about eight in the morning, and we were fired up and ready to go.

It was a beautiful Sunday morning just like I had prayed for. I was smiling from ear to ear as I climbed aboard bus "Number 1" of the First Foursquare Church bus ministry of Charlotte, North Carolina. Fred and I were both hyper. He was the designated driver, and I as the pastor just had to be along for this historic moment, but we first needed to pick up Ben at his house.

Fred and Ben were two very unique and gifted individuals. Fred and his wife Lib were searching for a church home that would accept them in spite of what they called "their baggage." Fred had served ten years in the Florida State Penitentiary for a series of robberies in regard to public telephone booths in the state of Florida. She was recovering from a broken marriage.

They had surrendered their lives to Christ but were both still deeply hurting from the failures of their pasts and needed genuine and loving support.

Ben was born and raised in Holland, and eventually became a United States Citizen. He was a very gifted artist. He, too, was recovering from a broken marriage and had admitted openly his past thoughts of suicide before He had accepted Christ.

We as a small but growing church family had decided that a bus ministry was one way in which we could continue to reach out to our community for the Lord. Inviting and bringing folks to church on a church bus was accelerating in numerous churches all across Charlotte. We had purchased this '60s model International bus from the Mecklenburg County School system, which had replaced it with a much a newer '70s bus. Our bus did need some patch up work and repainting, but it was actually in pretty good shape.

We had rented a spray-painting machine and had decided on fire engine red for the color of the bus. I had asked Ben, our own in-house Dutch artist, to paint a large white dove with wings expanded on each side of the bus. Of course we had the name of the church also painted in large white letters on both sides of the bus. I then asked Ben to paint a large number "1" on both the front and rear of the bus.

"Pastor, do you really think that we'll have more than one bus," he asked? "Ben, this bus is only the beginning for us," I responded reassuringly!

We only had seven people that we had picked up for church that morning, three teens and a family of four that wanted to be among the first passengers. We were not disappointed in the least. You should have seen the smiles upon all of our faces when we pulled into our small gravel parking lot. You would have thought that we had brought in more than half of the city of Charlotte for Sunday school and church.

Our small fifty-seat chapel was nearly full that Sunday, and to top it all off, we were headed to beautiful Lake Norman, located just north of Charlotte for a water baptismal. We had decided at the last minute to pack as many as possible into the bus for the short trip so we could enjoy the fellowship together. We were singing and clapping our hands joyfully in anticipation of baptizing twelve committed and excited individuals.

I was standing waist deep in the lake water and was comparing our twelve to be baptized to the twelve Disciples of Christ, whom had each decided to follow Him in obedience. We sang a few more choruses, and I then invited all twelve to come on in the water together. One by one they each carefully but cheerfully made their way into the water.

It was a moment that I will never forget. I was in the midst of a pastoral prayer over this special baptismal service, when all of a sudden I heard one of the male voices shout, "Oh!" and then a loud "Oh! Jesus!" I stopped momentarily, smiling on the inside and thinking that God's precious Holy Spirit had descended upon us.

I then heard a female voice shout, "Ouch! Ouch! It's biting me!" I opened my eyes to see several of them jumping up and down and trying to run out of the water.

"Oh! God help me!" shouted another, who had tripped and fallen face first into the lake. I could hear the despairing moans from the folks standing along the bank.

At this point I was dumfounded with my mouth wide open and no words able to come out. Near panic had now set in amongst those in the water. Folks were rushing in to the water in order to help get everyone out of the lake. After a few short minutes, I was the only one still standing in the water, but I had now moved to the waters edge. It was unbelievable. Some kind of small fish in large numbers had started nibbling the bare legs of our members. They had all come prepared for water baptism in shorts, and I was the only one with long pants on. I never felt a thing on my legs, but my mind sure was numb.

Well, after an hour of regaining our wits and courage, we began singing some more songs of praise, while several of us in long trousers splashed heartily in the water hoping to scare the fish away. We finally got those twelve disciples baptized. We were all laughing on the bus as we made our trip back to the church.

We had planned an evening service of celebration. Launching our bus ministry and baptizing twelve individuals in the waters of Lake Norman, in spite of the havoc, made that service a joyful time. One of our excited young people had even invited another young man off the street to that evening service. While the congregation was standing, we were singing and joyfully clapping our hands. This young man, positioned on the front row, was kind of rocking along with us. He then pulled a box of Cracker Jacks out of his hip pocket. He tore off the top of the box and thrust in a mouth full, and then continued rocking along with us. Well, it really annoyed me. I was thinking inwardly, "How could he be so disrespectful."

I'll never forget that moment. While we were continuing to sing enthusiastically, that hippy looking, smelly young man was determined to get the toy out of that box of Cracker Jacks. Oh, he loved our singing and for brief moments would place the box under his armpit and joyfully clap along with us, and then once again pursue that toy. Candied popcorn was now streaming onto the floor. It was just mind-boggling. I almost stepped over to help him. When he was finally successful in getting that toy, my mind shouted with relief, "Thank you, Lord!" His actions had distracted most of us, but as "good" church members, we continued to sing and clap our hands.

"Now what?" my mind screamed in distress as he began picking up the kernels off of the floor and stuffing them back into that box. This really stirred a contagious dislike for him, and I as the pastor was leading that growing animosity by my facial expressions. While the church was turning in their Bibles to the Scripture for my sermon, I was thinking, "How did our ushers let such a 'degenerate' not only get in our sanctuary door but make it to the front row?"

In all honesty, that sermon was the most unspiritual message that I had ever preached, but no one in the congregation cared or were even listening because their eyes were all on that "heathen" sitting on the front row. I closed the service with a quick altar call, hoping to get myself out of there before something else could happen, but that was too late. My head was bowed and my eyes were closed as I was closing in some unspiritual prayer when I heard the sound of weeping. I then completely froze. I didn't need to open my eyes in order to see who was weeping, I knew. My heart instantly broke. A hush descended over our sanctuary.

When was the last time that you remember making a decision that was wrong? Well, I knew at that precise moment that this pastor had miserably failed God at the conclusion of what had been an inspiring and historic day. In spite of my rejection as the pastor, that young man was kneeling at our humble wooden altar, weeping over the sins of his life. In spite of the rejection from that church family, that young man laid his box of Cracker Jacks down on that altar and was humbly kneeling before God.

I just couldn't believe it. We had launched our bus ministry that very morning in hopes of reaching our community for Christ. We had then assembled our church family together and spent that entire afternoon rejoicing over twelve individuals who had recently accepted Christ into their lives and witnessed their obedience to Him in water baptism. After a day like that, how could we have totally and completely rejected someone like we did?

I knelt beside that young man, but I wasn't praying for him. I was praying for me. I, too, could not hold back the tears as I prayerfully reflected upon my pitiful actions that evening. Initiating the bus ministry and baptizing twelve individuals was all completely in vain if this was to be the attitude of this pastor and congregation. I repented that night and made my second covenant vow to God. My first vow being that I would remain a faithful husband to my beautiful bride, Claudia. This second vow was very clear in my mind and heart. "God, I promise you, never again will I reject someone like I have tonight. I promise!"

Thankfully, our actions that historic night did not override the work of the Holy Spirit. God showed us His forgiveness and amazing grace during the coming months as that young man named Clay became more and more impassioned in his walk with God.

He had actually gone to a local Christian bookstore and purchased a large coffee-table-type Bible for his own personal use. He said he wanted his friends to know that he was not ashamed to be a Christian. Every Sunday I would smile when I would watch him lug that big Bible into church. He would then prop it up on his crossed leg and hold it securely in order to keep it from slipping to the floor, as he would faithfully follow the pastor's sermon Scripture references. Clay actually became one of our most energetic and compassionate youth leaders.

Another significant day in my life was when Steve and I were sitting in one of the work vans of Metrolina Contracting & Cleaning. We were eating lunch at the McDonalds located on Freedom Drive in Charlotte, North Carolina. We had the radio turned up and tuned in to the only local Christian radio station. I was so nervous that Steve had to keep trying to settle me down. You see, this was my very first radio broadcast. Through a number of events over the past few months, Claudia and I and our small church family had decided to take this step to reach out to the men and women of our city.

It was a leap of faith for us, but we all felt so strongly that this was in God's will. We had signed a one-year contract with radio station WHVN-1350-AM. It was mostly local churches and pastors broadcasting on a daily basis. In my thinking, we were given a key time slot for our radio broadcast. It was during the lunch time on Tuesdays and Thursdays from 12:35 to 1 p.m. We named our program *The Old Time Revival Hour*. Even now, it brings a smile to my face that this young and energetic pastor would reference his life and ministry on the radio as "Old Time." I was twenty-four years old with very little experience in the ministry and absolutely no experience in the media. Oh, I was an eager listener to these local established pastors and had received much from their teaching and preaching, and I knew that there were many others throughout this large bustling city like me.

However, there had been quite a warfare going on between those pastors on the subject of "speaking in other tongues." It was sad and yet somewhat comical to hear one speak on, "Why I do not speak in other tongues," and the next scheduled pastor would invariably speak on, "Why I do speak in other tongues." I did not want to get into that controversial battle over the airwaves.

My decision then was to begin our very first twenty-five-minute broadcast with a story from the life of Christ and then continue with various other stories from His life in subsequent broadcasts. I was to discover almost immediately that the listening audience in that metropolitan city was ready for somebody, anybody, even a *nobody* to "please" talk and teach on something else. Well, I fit the *nobody* category, but somehow knew that the Lord had placed this media gift within my life.

The overall picture was kind of strange. Here I was working this outside job and listening to myself teach on Christian radio. There simply wasn't enough money in our church for me to receive a reasonable salary, so I accepted this for however long it would be necessary. This new job, after leaving the sandwich company, was going to become quite a fruitful mission field for me in the coming months.

Steve and I made our way on to our newest job assignment. We were both very nervous and apprehensive. We had been asked to begin the cleanup at a house in the southern part of Charlotte where a double murder had recently taken place. This tragedy had been in the headlines of the local newspapers and on television and radio. It was a bizarre murder of an older husband and wife in their home. The police had captured the brutal killer, and the house, as a crime scene under investigation, had been cleared for us to enter.

As we entered the house, we were immediately impacted by the foul odor. We stopped and looked at each other with a despondent stare. We slowly made our way to the hallway leading to the rear of the house where the murders had been committed. Again we both stopped as we stared at the large pool of dried blood on the carpet as well as what was splattered on the walls and ceiling. The hallway is where the husband was shot to death. He had placed his wife in the bathroom where he had tried to barricade the door and protect her. We saw the bathroom door lying in an adjoining bedroom. It had several bullet holes in it and had been partially ripped off by the cruel intruder. The wife had been viciously killed in the bathroom.

As Steve and I carefully walked across the hallway and looked at the splattering of blood over the toilet, sink, walls and floor; we both rushed back outside to the backyard. I fell on my knees just off the porch and vomited several times. I slowly looked up to see Steve continually heaving as he huddled close to a nearby bush.

It took us about an hour to recover. We discussed quitting our jobs, but gradually encouraged each other that we could do this. We decided to take fifteen-minute intervals, one of us cleaning while the other stayed outside in the fresh air. Those three days were long and very emotional days.

On our final day at the house, the family came, along with a police escort. Thankfully they did not have to see or smell what we had as we dealt with the totally miserable mess, but that didn't take away the sorrow and grief that they each openly displayed. One of the daughters, about my age, collapsed in the hallway floor as she glared into the bathroom. No one could say anything that could erase the pain. The police officer took off his hat in respect. I sat down on the floor beside her and just held her hand as she wept. It was a scene that I will never forget.

If that was not enough emotion for one week, I received a

phone call from a funeral home director asking me to conduct a funeral for a man that had committed suicide. All the way to the funeral home I was feeling an emotional spiral downward. This had been such a negative week.

Going over and over in my mind was my conversation with the funeral home director. He had asked several other pastors to conduct the funeral, but all of them had declined. I was thinking, "That's what I should have done, just say the simple word 'No'!" However, when he described a weeping mother wanting a "preacher" to say the final words over her dead son, I just could not find the word "No."

It was another heartbreaking scene. I sat beside this mother in the depths of pain and anguish. We were positioned in front of the open casket. She would keep reaching up and touching his folded hands and then briefly recite another story in her raising him.

He was in his thirties and married with young children. He had an affair. According to his final handwritten note, he loved both women and couldn't see any other way out. He had duct taped a garden hose to his car's exhaust pipe and worked it around through his front seat window and then started the engine. He died alone, locked in his car that was inside his garage.

As I stood beside the now closed casket, facing the small gathering of family, my heart ached for his small children. His wife and kids sat to the far right on the front row. All of them were crying. The lady with whom he had the affair with was sitting to the far left on the front row, stone-faced. His mother was sitting front and center, continually weeping.

My words were few. I recited Psalm 23 and then read a portion of the fourteenth chapter of the Gospel of John. *"Let not your heart be troubled; you believe in God, believe also in Me.*" I prayed for God's peace and then escorted the casket to the cemetery.

That week was a historic and monumental week for me personally. I had taken steps of faith to reach out to the city in which I was a pastor. Steps to teach thousands of listeners to Christian radio about the Savior of the world, Jesus Christ. Steps to bring Christ's peace to a few who were deeply hurting as a result of the strategies of our ruthless adversary, the devil.

Chapter 7

PRAYER THAT BREAKS THROUGH

"My help comes from the Lord, who made heaven and earth."
Psalm 121:2

You have to understand why I was so nervous. After two-and-a-half years of pastoring a small congregation, this particular day, I was nervously sweating. With every sermon being preached in a small fifty-seat chapel, this day, I was near panic. I was now standing behind the pulpit in a sanctuary that seated over five hundred people, and most of them were present. This was my second opportunity to preach to this large congregation.

Claudia and I had traveled to her home for Christmas. New Castle, Indiana was a small town located east of the capitol of Indiana, the bustling city of Indianapolis. It was cold, and they were expecting more winter weather. This historic day was Sunday morning, December 24, 1972. Pastor Flowers had asked me to preach in this Christmas Eve morning service. He desired to honor us and had requested that Claudia lead the morning worship. We were married in this New Castle Foursquare Church on Saturday, July 26, 1969.

Claudia had accepted Christ at age thirteen, a result of the Godly influence of this church family. In the following years she would become one of their outstanding teen leaders. Claudia would grow spiritually and ultimately impact her own family. Her faith and walk with God was instrumental in her brother, Larry, coming to Christ. Her influence upon her parents was significant. After her graduation from Chrysler High School in 1967, and one year of her working to save money, her parents would then tearfully send her off to Mount Vernon Bible College. She was endeavoring to follow the call of God upon her life.

As I stood there in that pulpit nervously preaching a sermon entitled *Steadfast In Christ*, the invisible hand of God was reaching down in order to change the lives of Tim and Claudia Kelton, forever. We are indebted to the Holy Spirit's quickening power within the lives of God's people, a debt that we can never repay. Every now and then when I find myself discouraged, I remember that historic Christmas Eve morning in 1972.

At the close of my message, I extended an invitation to anyone present that desired to personally know Jesus Christ to please step from his or her pew and make their way to the altar. To my pleasant surprise, several people walked to the front of that sanctuary for prayer. Pastor Flowers and I stepped down from the platform in order to pray with those men and women.

Being distracted by additional and very audible prayers other than our own, I looked across the sanctuary from where we were standing at a group of folks circled around Claudia. My initial thought was that this group, mostly ladies, was demonstrating their love and compassion for Claudia who had grown up amongst them. My observation was correct, but only partially. A truly God-inspired miracle from heaven was taking place in my wife.

A well-respected leader within that church family looked me in the eyes as he clarified what had taken place. "You might think that I'm crazy when I tell you this, but while Claudia was leading worship, I saw a dark misty cloud over Claudia's stomach." With intensity he continued. "I became so alarmed by what I saw and by what I was sensing, that I nearly interrupted the service several times."

I just stood there gazing at this man as he continued to speak to us. "I knew that Claudia was in trouble, and as soon as you opened the altars for prayer, I gathered these women to join me in earnest prayer for her." I could visually see Claudia weeping as my eyes and ears turned back to this trembling man. "As we were just now praying over her, that dark misty cloud disappeared!" My heart was now pounding. His final tearful words were, "It's gone! I don't know what this means, but that cloud is not there. It's gone!"

Now over three decades later, I can still hear Claudia's weeping voice. I can still see those precious ladies gathered around her and intently praying for her. I remember wiping the tears away as they trickled down my cheeks. As though it happened yesterday, I can still hear that obedient servant of God saying, "It's gone!" I remember thinking, "God, can it be that Tim and Claudia Kelton have truly received a miracle from You?"

Claudia knew. I knew. No one else but God and the doctors knew that we were unable to have children. We had been in the midst of in-depth testing, and the results were revealing the very painful reality that Claudia could not bear children. With every fiber of faith within us, we as a couple had prayed that God would make a way for us to be able to have our own children. To our eyes and ears it did not seem possible, but our hearts had been praying and yearning for God to make a way where there seemed to be no way. We were a couple that desperately wanted to have children. Well, you can look at a calendar or count on your fingers that first miracle day.

On September 13, 1973, Angela Sue was born! In those days, fathers generally were not allowed near the birthing process. Claudia's parents and my mother were present with me in the waiting room. I was so anxious and tense that I just could not stop rotating back and forth in that crazy chair. They all kept chuckling at my actions.

Then it happened. That stupid swivel chair broke, and I remember it was like I was in slow motion as I floated to the waiting room floor. Claudia's dad rarely laughed, but I'm telling you that he could not stop laughing at that whole scene. After positioning myself in another chair and nervously watching for that phone in the waiting room of the Charlotte Presbyterian Hospital to finally ring, the nurse then held that naked newborn baby up for me to see. With great emotion, I just stared at that beautiful, miracle baby girl through the glass. She was yawning, already bored with life.

On August 9, 1977, Valerie Lynne was born! I had been given a very difficult assignment. Sit with two extremely emotional and anxious grandmothers while waiting for the birth of our second baby. I would not wish that assignment on anyone. Thinking that we had several more hours of waiting, Granny Mary, Grandma Myda and I had made our way to the cafeteria of the Charlotte Memorial Hospital in order to eat breakfast. After one of the staff had ordered me to an in-house telephone in the cafeteria, I made my mad rush back to the maternity floor. While standing anxiously trying to get someone's attention at the nurse's station, I saw Claudia being moved into a room. I quickly made my way to her, where she was momentarily stopped in the hallway. I'll never forget that moment. I leaned over the bed to kiss Claudia and said, "What do we have here?"

With a weak smile, Claudia gently rolled back the soft nursery blanket that enveloped our second beautiful, miracle baby girl. Maybe it's just a very proud dad boasting, but I promise you, Valerie turned her head immediately toward the sound of my voice.

On July 7, 1981, Jonathan Paul was born! For some reason, Presbyterian Hospital could not find a hospital gown that would fit me. Yes, I was six feet two inches tall, but I wasn't that hefty. I was "only" two hundred sixty pounds. Oh well, they fitted one of those green hospital gowns around me from the back and then one from the front. It was a little embarrassing.

After hearing that we were expecting for the third time, Claudia's mom and dad said, "We hope you are not going to fill up the backyard with girls while trying to have a boy." That wasn't the case at all. Our hearts were saying, "God, please allow us to have the children that you want for our lives." However, experiencing a boy after eight years of two feminine girls definitely presented us with an abundance of new challenges. Nevertheless, we have rejoiced with grateful hearts over the birth of that handsome son, our third miracle baby.

Now on another historic day, nothing could wipe the smile off of my face after the phone call from the General Manager of WHVN-1350 AM, inquiring if we were ready to take on two additional days for our broadcast. "We just received notification that the church who has been with us for several years with their broadcast on Mondays and Fridays has decided not to renew their annual contract," Tom Gentry gently spoke. "You do know, Tim, that their broadcasts are at the same identical time as yours."

I couldn't believe it. In less than one year I would be able to teach on the radio four days a week, from 12:35 to 1 p.m. Without any prayer or in-depth consideration about such a huge step, I replied excitedly, "Yes, Tom! We'll take it!"

He then closed our conversation with a hearty "Congratulations, Tim! I would have never thought things would be so positive for you and your church family."

He then said, "Tim, the prospect of you getting the Wednesday time slot from Victory Baptist Church is very slim. They have been broadcasting on that day at the noon time for many years." "That's okay," I said, and then rushed to tell Claudia the exciting news. Of course, I was pretty sobered in the next few hours, days and months as the full picture became more clear to my mind. The weekly bill would now jump from fifty dollars to one hundred dollars, as well as the time and effort to prepare four twenty-five-minute daily broadcasts per week along with my growing pastoral responsibilities. Well, the smile never left, but my life would be changed.

It was truly one of the most fulfilling seasons of my life and ministry. Our radio program, *The Old Time Revival Hour*, was touching a nerve within the listening audience. I had been committed to teaching on principles for Christian living; many of those were from the various stories within the life of Christ. We were so excited and yet deeply humbled at the continued response from our daily broadcast. Our key time slot for our broadcast during lunchtime was very advantageous.

However, I was struggling with the task of preparing for and producing those daily twenty-five-minute broadcasts. As any pastor would desire, I wanted each broadcast to be sharp, to the point and viable for every listening ear. It was like teaching four Sunday sermons during the week, to be followed by a Sunday sermon, to only begin again on Monday with four more Sunday sermons, to be followed by, well, you get the picture. I had no staff. I was the radio preacher and teacher while heading up the Theology and Biblical Analysis Departments, the Historical Research Department, and serving as the Director of Operations and Senior Editor, followed by the responsibility of production and Senior Audio Technician, and then of course, the Special Courier, making sure the programs made it to the radio station. I remember thinking one day, while en-route with that week's taped broadcasts; *It's no wonder that the nearly five hundred pastors within the city of Charlotte did not have a daily broadcast!*

However, we were seeing the results of those daily broadcasts nearly every week with letters from listeners acknowledging encouragement. I was amazed that some listeners would acknowledge conviction within a certain area of their life and ask for additional counsel or help. All a result of just one daily radio broadcast!

I was also amazed at the listeners who were making their way to our small congregation, situated on the outskirts of the city. They would drive by numerous beautiful church facilities that had been established for years, to make their way to our humble farmhouse that had been renovated into a fifty-seat chapel with a small gravel parking area. As the church grew numerically, they would have to park in the grass. Please know that I understood clearly that I was a *nobody* and that it had little to do with me, and much to do with God's gift upon us.

One of the most memorable early responses from the radio ministry was a visit to our midweek Bible study by Henry. He was gentle and very hungry for the things of God. We were to discover that he was the vice-president of a local bank. He was a member of a very large church that had been established for over one hundred years. Henry was also very encouraging as to our daily radio broadcasts. He told me that he would seek to schedule his lunch break at the bank so he would not miss the broadcast.

I had heard of a Messianic Jew, Marvin Aranove, who had been a very successful businessman and was now traveling across the country sharing his personal testimony of salvation. He was preaching in both large and small congregations. I invited him for a full week of special meetings. He never hesitated when I explained to him that our church was small and situated on the outskirts of Charlotte.

That week, which turned into two weeks with this Jewish evangelist, not only changed my life, but would also change the lives of many who came to those special meetings. We also went "live" from the radio studios during our daily broadcasts. Many people made their way to our church as a result. The testimonies were in abundance as to the results of those two weeks of "live" radio broadcasts.

Henry had invited a businessman that he had been dealing with at the bank. This man was on the brink of bankruptcy and was deeply depressed. The night that Henry and Bob walked in was also the night that one of our excited young people had invited a beautiful young lady to church. She was also despondent. She told us that her friends called her "Sunshine." Believe me; that would have been the last nickname that we would have chosen for her. The opposite of "sunshine" was how she looked!

After hearing the personal testimony of this Jewish preacher, Sunshine stepped forward, asking us to pray for her. We had just taken hold of her hands in an attitude of prayer when she collapsed to the floor and began writhing and twisting. I was shocked, but I had seen and heard some of this while in prayer for my brother David. After a time of prayer, this young woman just laid on the floor. In time, she arose a new person. She confessed to us that she had been determined to take her life because she could not bear the pain of her life any longer. She surrendered to Christ! She now looked like "sunshine!"

Henry and Bob had witnessed this event with Sunshine. That night was to be a life changing night for Bob, too, who also accepted Christ as his personal Savior. He admitted to us that he possessed a handgun and had determined to end his life that night as well.

The results of that one single night were amazing. Two individuals who were both suicidal ended up at the same address and were confronted by the same compassionate God of the Bible. Their lives, destinies and families were to be forever changed.

Sunshine came to church the very next Sunday. She was in a micro-mini skirt and see-thru blouse and was smiling from ear to ear. Most of the guys about fell out of their seats! Claudia, along with several of our ladies, began to teach her about dressing more modestly, which she immediately began to respond to. It was a day mixed with tears and smiles when she packed up to return to her family living in another city as a "prodigal" returning home.

Bob and his wife Vicki had become faithful members in our congregation. Little did we know, but that in the not-too-distant future, Bob, who was an architect, would not only draw up the plans for our new 400-seat sanctuary, but also help to construct it; and in the coming years, he and his wife would become prominent pastors in the metropolitan region of Richmond, Virginia, sowing the seed for one of their sons-in-law to join them in ministry.

Henry, his wife Jeannie and their young teenage son Bryan also became dedicated and loving members in our church family. This son would grow up to become a devoted father to his own wife and children, as well as serve Christ as a staff pastor in another church family within the state of North Carolina.

I never cease to be amazed at how one decision, one obedient step, one sacrificial action, can have such far reaching and long term ramifications; especially in God's work! Look what a decision to go on the radio and teach about the life of Christ resulted in. Look what a decision to invite a gifted individual to the pulpit of a small church on the outskirts of a large city resulted in. Thank God for His ever-abundant mercy in our lives!

Chapter 8

LET GOD STAY IN CONTROL

*"And whatever you do, do it heartily, as to the Lord and not
to men, knowing that from the Lord you will receive the
reward of the inheritance, for you serve the Lord Christ."*
Colossians 4:23,24

It was a heart-wrenching disappointment in myself, but I had
at least completed what I knew that God had called me to. The
disappointment was that I had been through four years of college, but only had enough credits to graduate with the three-year
"Standard Ministerial Diploma." I wanted the Bachelor of Theology Degree along with the "Advanced Ministerial Diploma,"
but I decided to press on into the ministry. The disappointment
was replaced with deep joy when I saw my name on that diploma.
I was the first of my family to graduate from college.

The joy was increased when Claudia and I received our
first pastoral appointment to Charlotte, North Carolina. We
had been serving there since July 1970, and had worked very
hard. We had launched our small but growing church into a bus
ministry. We were seeing numerous responses from our daily
twenty-five-minute radio broadcast. We were rejoicing over the
lives that we had seen changed. Our church family had asked us
to quit our outside jobs and trust the Lord for our finances. We

had just received the news that we were expecting our first baby. We were excited. We were tired. We were humbled.

We were now excited about another momentous event in our lives; it was my ordination. Claudia and I were in the midst of making plans to travel for ordination to Los Angeles, the International Headquarters of our denomination. I was finally eligible for ordination at this 1973 convention, our first International Foursquare Convention that we would be privileged to attend. It was a day of great joy and deep fulfillment.

My sister Marquita and her husband Duane had linked us with their pastor at the First Assembly of God in Excelsior Springs, Missouri, who had extended to us an invitation to lead a one-week revival meeting in the church. We had driven to Missouri, parked our car and then caught a flight to Los Angeles for that special ordination service. Then upon our return, we stayed with Marquita and Duane for the week of services. That decision was to be life-changing.

Pastor Al had served at the church for a number of years. He was a good-hearted and gifted man. His family was talented, and they were all truly committed to not only that church family but to the community. However, the congregation was struggling.

As that week of special nightly services moved forward, the church family was very unresponsive. I was teaching on truths that I had been learning and experiencing in my own life as a young pastor, especially in the realm of spiritual battle and warfare. I had shared some of our own recent experiences as a pastor, such as the split in our young church as a result of my referring too much to the devil in my preaching. My brother David's deliverance and conversion from sixteen years of addictions was one of my topics. I continued the best that I could until the final Sunday night service, but it had been a very difficult week.

To this day, I still do not fully comprehend what happened in that final service. Before I could finish the teaching on Christ's authority over all other powers, a man ran down the middle aisle of the sanctuary and fell on his knees at the altar. He was weeping audibly while saying repeatedly, "God, forgive me!" He was one of the elders of that church. Others across the sanctuary began crying, while yet others would moan. Some stood to their feet, weeping, while many others made their way to the altar of that sanctuary. No invitation had been given, but I tearfully and thankfully understood that my part was over. It was now God's Spirit doing His part. It was truly amazing. This went on for nearly an hour. Pastor Al was moving across the sanctuary from person to person while often looking heavenward with a huge smile upon his face and joyful praise sounding from his lips.

He made his way to the platform where I was standing. "My brother, I have been praying for this day for many years. Please! Please stay and finish what God has started!"

Claudia and I could not find the word "no." We consented to staying for one more week. That single decision was to mark our lives and the lives of many people forever. I am to this day still amazed at how God chose to work through a young and inexperienced couple like us. We were so humbled.

Our church family back in Charlotte was also amazed. We prayerfully committed to that second week and would not actually return home until completing seven weeks. We communicated with them nearly every day. They were a part of this miracle. Our leaders took turns covering the Sunday services and the midweek Bible study.

I was challenged to producing our daily twenty-five-minute radio broadcasts and shipping them from Missouri to the radio station in North Carolina every week. I had only prepared three weeks of broadcasts in advance in order to cover our scheduled time to be gone. Pre-recorded radio programs in the early seventies were placed on a seven-inch reel-to-reel tape. I made several trips to the closest Radio Shack electronics store for purchasing two dozen more tapes. It was an exhausting and life-changing time for all of us.

Pastor Al was such a unique and gifted individual. His smile never ceased during those seven weeks. He kept saying to me, "This only happens once in a lifetime!"

It never seemed to bother him that I was a Foursquare preacher in his Assembly of God church. It didn't seem to distress him that I was only twenty-five and inexperienced and he was a seasoned pastor. He just kept saying, "Please, don't leave until God has finished his work here!"

Even today as I reflect over the numerous stories and testimonies resulting from those seven weeks, it brings tears to my eyes. One of the key leaders within that church family had openly repented as to an affair that he had been involved in at his job. Another key member had become addicted to alcohol and confessed her battle. One young woman openly remorsed over her continued past thoughts of suicide, a result of an ongoing struggle with her husband's aggressive addiction to pornography. Another couple repented of their passive behavior toward their marriage relationship. They had been slowly drifting apart. She had even become curiously caught up with elements of "witchcraft" and had started drinking cocktails before she would return home from her daily job. These two were very respected leaders in this church.

Claudia and I had been as faithful to the Lord as we knew how. I had stood in that pulpit for forty-three days in a row. As the guest preacher, counting two sermons each Sunday of those first six weeks, I had brought forty-nine messages from the Bible and from the heart.

During all of this, Claudia had struggled greatly in those first months of her pregnancy. Several nights as I was preaching in the sanctuary, Pastor Al and his wife would escort Claudia to the basement restrooms where she would continually throw up and try to cope with her ongoing battle of nausea and queasiness.

However, we both had this pounding sense that we shouldn't leave before dedicating a week of ministry to children. So the seventh week of those special meetings was billed as a "Kid's Crusade," postured around *The King's Castle*. Claudia and her amazing artistic abilities, in spite of her physical battle, helped us design and create a huge colorful plywood castle accompanied by *Pokey* the singing elephant; *Squire Pup* the primary puppet spokesman; and many other puppet characters. The *King's Treasure Chest* that was always full of goodies for each night was a big hit with the kids. The children came in droves, bringing their friends. Buses and vans from numerous other churches joined in as well. It was great!

Then Pastor Al decided that he wanted to break their attendance record and joyfully announced that he and the guest preacher would eat steaming fried chicken on the rooftop of the church if they would break their record attendance of 248. He then nervously whispered to me, "That is okay with you? Right? Huh, what did you say?" I'm being honest with you; I have never yet answered that pastor about such a wacky event.

Well, on that historic final Sunday, they reached their new

record attendance of 252. I heard later that one of the ushers had rushed out on to the street and offered four teenage boys one dollar each if they would attend church that morning and help them break the record. With a reporter present from the local newspaper, Pastor Al and I climbed a ladder to the top of the church building and ate our steaming fried chicken. Yep, as you might have suspected, our pictures made the newspaper.

One of the key decisions upon our return to Charlotte was the fulfillment of the vision that God had given us as a church family to develop a 24-hour telephone prayer line. We were still a small congregation in comparison to many churches around us, but that didn't seem to hinder our final decision. With great determination, we rolled up our sleeves and began.

It did take some time to get an additional telephone line connected and start the process of training many of our church members who were excited about being a part of this new ministry within our church and community. We settled on the name "Life Line," with each of those eight letters representing our goal and mission.

Look at yourself.
Is your life filled with the happiness that you need?
Freedom has a price, are you willing to pay it?
Everyone can have happiness and freedom. The price has already been paid.
Look to Jesus!
In Him only will you find all your answers.
Nowhere else can the way, the truth or the life be found.
Everyone who seeks the truth will find that Jesus is the only answer.

With several weeks of training behind us, along with paid advertising within two local newspapers and the local Christian radio station, the first day of ministry had begun. We were unable to schedule the entire 24-hour day with volunteers, but we were covering the phone from 6 a.m. until midnight. We recorded over one hundred phone calls in the first three weeks. By the end of the first month we had all 24 hours covered with our church members and volunteers.

It was an amazing experience. Even the local newspapers were asking to feature stories pertaining to our counselors as well as the 24-hour prayer line itself. We maintained this ministry for over a year, until we were forced to tear down our church building and begin construction of a new sanctuary.

I was pleasantly surprised and encouraged as a number of individuals made their way to our church as a result of receiving spiritual help and counsel on the prayer line. It was also very encouraging to see the spiritual growth of so many of our volunteer counselors. Several of our church members expressed that their hours devoted to the prayer line had changed their lives. One of them even explained how they saw their time in the prayer room and on the prayer phone was like committing their life to God during a time of "fasting." When I asked them to clarify their thinking to me, they explained that they were fasting hours of sitting in front of their television at home.

Chapter 9

A Light In A World Of Darkness

"When it goes well with the righteous, the city rejoices."
Proverbs *11:10*a

It was late summer in the year 1973. Claudia and I had just celebrated our fourth wedding anniversary and our third anniversary as pastors of the First Foursquare Church, 6800 The Plaza, in the bustling city of Charlotte, North Carolina. We had no idea just how much our lives and ministry were going to change. We were in for a very wild ride.

I was absolutely breathless when I hung up the telephone. My mind was in shock. Once again I found myself in another situation beyond my comprehension, because I could not find the word "no."

"Honey, what's wrong," Claudia nervously inquired? My mouth was so dry I could hardly speak a response. "Tim, what's the matter?" she continued to probe. I finally answered her, "Claudia, I'm going to be on T.V."

Our eyes just stared at each other. "What do you mean," she asked? "That telephone call was from a woman named Alice. She said that Jim and Tammy Bakker were starting a television show in Charlotte, and I was invited to be the first guest to be interviewed." Claudia's mouth just widened as she stared at me.

"Claudia, we have been invited to a picnic with the Bakker's and some of their staff next weekend."

Alice had briefly related to me that the reason they had invited me to be a guest was a result of our daily noontime radio program. I responded to her that I had never been on television and I knew nothing about television. She gently responded, "Rev. Kelton, Jim and Tammy just want to talk to you about your Christian experience, that's all." Why I just didn't say "no thank you," I will never understand.

Advertising was widespread throughout the city of Charlotte about the *Trinity Broadcasting Praise The Lord Show* to be televised on WRET, Channel 36, an independent television station owned and operated by a man that few of us knew about at that time. His name was Ted Turner. The studios were located on the outskirts of the city. We were stunned when we realized that it was only a few miles from the location of our church.

When we arrived at the picnic we realized that we didn't know anyone. There were a number of Christian businessmen of which one was the General Manager of WRET, Channel 36. We were very impressed with this man, Sandy Wheeler, and his wife Martha. After listening to their communications, there was no doubt in our hearts that they were committed to touching that growing city for Christ.

After everyone had finished eating, Sandy Wheeler asked us all to gather closer together for a time of dialogue. Claudia and I became very nervous as the exchange within this small group of people became more and more centered upon us. Yes, we had a daily twenty-five-minute radio broadcast, but it was only in its second year. Yes, we were pastoring a growing church of sixty to seventy people, but we were only three years into the ministry. Yes, it was true that we launched a bus ministry with two bright red buses with large white doves on the sides, but we were relatively new to this type of outreach ministry. Yes, it was joyfully true that Claudia was seven months pregnant with our first miracle child due in September.

"Tim and Claudia, as you have already seen, Jim and Tammy are not with us this evening," Sandy Wheeler gently spoke. "This is our dilemma. Jim and Tammy are in California and will be unable to get here for our scheduled opening night. In fact, they say it will probably be a couple of weeks before they can get here." He continued speaking while clearly he and the others were looking directly at us. "We have spent thousands of dollars on advertising. A lot of people have diligently been preparing for this historic moment in our city. We all agree that we would like to stay on track and on schedule. So, we are asking you, brother, would you help us by taking the leadership and hosting our programs over the next few weeks until Jim and Tammy arrive?" He then became silent, with a smile upon his kind face.

I know it will sound crazy, but the only way I can describe my inner emotions at that moment is it was like an instant flashback of me as a little boy trying to learn how to tumble so I could get a Cub Scout Badge. While running, I jumped forward trying to tuck my head under, but failed. Instead, I landed directly on the top of my head, breaking my neck and was hospitalized. All I could see was stars. I'll tell you the rest of that story some other time.

Well, it was a good thing that I was sitting down, because all I could see was stars and I wasn't seeing Hollywood Stars. I was seeing fuzzy, blurry stars. My heart was racing from near panic. Then it happened! That youthful, immature, green, unseasoned, still wet behind the ears Tim Kelton opened his big mouth and spoke with a certain authority, "We shouldn't delay. We shouldn't waste the money. We should start as scheduled."

There was an immediate reaction of relief and excitement. We could hear various voices within that small group of people joyfully praising the Lord in agreement.

On that historic Sunday night, I was the only one "not" praising the Lord as the clock continued to count down for the very first *Praise The Lord Show*. We were going "live" at 10 p.m. from the studios of WRET, channel 36. The three cameras and crew were all set. The studios were jammed full of excited people. There were two banks of telephones with joyful people anticipating their first phone calls from viewers. A popular singing group called *The Downings* had finished warming up and was anxiously waiting in the wings.

Sandy Wheeler escorted me to the center of the small platform as he gently encouraged me to look directly into the central camera when I spoke. He then escorted Tom Bailey, the co-host, a tenderhearted Christian businessman who built small yachts for a living, to stand beside me. We were both sweating as we stood nervously underneath the heat of at least two-dozen television studio lights. One of the staff held up a cue card with the hand-written words, "60 SECONDS." Then a hush came over the people in the studio.

We had been told that a musical opening with a professional voice would introduce the *Praise The Lord Show*. What we weren't told was that they did not have enough time to update the introduction and make the needed changes. Those 60 seconds went by swiftly!

A hand in motion, situated beneath the lens of that central camera, signaled us with five extended fingers … then four …

then three ... then two ... and then suddenly the musical introduction began. That booming professional voice clearly articulated the joyful introduction, "Welcome to the *Praise The Lord Show!* Now, here's ... Jim and Tammy Bakker!"

I was completely stunned! I had spent hours meditating on what my opening words would be and in just five seconds, with a dazed brain, my opening was, "Uh ... well ... obviously you can see that ... uh ... we are not Jim and Tammy Bakker."

I could hear chuckles everywhere. "My name is Tim Kelton and this is... uh ..." and then Tom softly interjected, "I'm Tom Bailey."

I rapidly spoke about Jim and Tammy being in California, and that we had telephone counselors ready to take the viewers phone calls and then a few other disjointed phrases about Christian Television now having a local base within our community, saying everything in my weary, drained, baffled and confused mind in about fifteen minutes.

I then just stopped. I looked up at the clock on the studio wall and thought inwardly. "My Lord, this is a two hour show. I'm wasted!" I quickly introduced the singing group, *The Downings,* and finally the cameras focused on them on the other side of the studio as they began joyfully singing. So went my debut in Christian television.

My involvement in Christian television was to only be for a brief season. I still do not fully understand all that transpired in those few months, but I quickly discerned the spiritual battle for the media airwaves. Through my involvement, I witnessed intense tension between some of the top leaders in Christian television from across the nation. Frankly, I was not only greatly surprised but also deeply embarrassed on many occasions, and that was only in the beginning years of the 1970s. I matured rapidly as a young pastor.

Tom Bailey and I co-hosted together the first months of the daily *Praise The Lord Show*. It was "live" Monday thru Friday, from 11 a.m. to 1 p.m. and then "live" every Sunday night for two hours, beginning at 10 p.m. Many local pastors, as well as various spiritual leaders throughout the region, were invited as guests. My most meaningful memory was the day I interviewed Corrie Ten Boom, known internationally as a result of her confinement in a Nazi concentration camp. I truly sat in the presence of Jesus Christ that day. I have always been grateful for the experiences of those few months.

One Christian businessman gently responded to my question, "Why me? Why, Tom?" He explained that I was young and inexperienced and offered no threat to local leaders. I still remember his grin when he reminded me about the broken down farm house that I had for a church building that was no threat to the local churches. Tom was a gentle, laid-back boat builder. "You two are just what the Lord needed," he softly interjected. *"God has chosen the foolish things of the world to put to shame the wise"* (I Corinthians 1:27).

My second most meaningful memory during those television days was after the birth of our first miracle baby, Angela Sue. The ministry staff wanted Claudia and to tell the story of our answered prayers to start a family. As I'm writing this, over three decades later, I'm still shaking my head in disbelief. When Claudia stepped onto the set with that beaming smile of hers, holding our precious newborn baby, her smile quickly faded. I learned later, that as the cameras zoomed in for a close-up view of Angela, she filled her diaper.

In November of 1973, Jim and Tammy Bakker began making their decision to leave California and move to Charlotte. It was a nervous but exciting moment for all of us local folks when Jim sat in the host's seat on that very first day in Charlotte. As I took the co-host seat, Jim and I shook hands and quickly greeted each other. In minutes, we were "on the air." There was no doubt in my heart that Jim Bakker was supposed to be there.

Several weeks later I withdrew from the television ministry. I had fulfilled my brief assignment from the Lord. On many occasions, Jim showed his appreciation to Claudia and me. When he had heard that we had torn down that old farmhouse church at 6800 The Plaza and were endeavoring to build our new sanctuary, he appealed to the viewing audience to send a "one-dollar" gift to our church address. Over $5,000 came through the mail in one-dollar gifts, accompanied by many hand-written prayers and thank you notes for our small part in birthing Christian television in the Charlotte area. On that memorable dedication Sunday in December of 1975, Jim stood behind the pulpit of our new four hundred-seat sanctuary.

One of Tammy Bakker's friends asked me to allow Tammy to slip in to our Sunday evening services without me making a big deal in recognizing her. My response was, "Okay." She asked if I was still teaching on Psalm 23. I affirmed that I was. She said that Tammy had heard about that current teaching and was hoping to receive from those words.

My heart is deeply saddened today when I think on all that was accomplished, followed by the tragic decisions of so many. Both the good and the bad left its unbelievable mark on both the church world as well as our country.

NOTE: From that single studio at WRET-TV on the outskirts of Charlotte, to a furniture store on East Independence Boulevard, then to the opposite side of Charlotte, with the final destination at Heritage U.S.A. near Fort Mill, South Carolina, came numerous testimonies of encouragement from the viewing audience. Thousands of lives were greatly strengthened through the *PTL Ministry.*

As a result of my brief role in the very beginning of the *PTL Ministry,* reporters from several newspapers contacted me for my take on the tragedy of Jim Bakker's imprisonment. I declined interviews with all of them, except one. After an initial lengthy conversation with Charles E. Shepard, a reporter for the *Charlotte Observer* newspaper, I consented to a four-hour telephone interview. He promised me that he would only write what I consented to. After reading his book, I can say that he kept his word to me. In a future book, I will convey those stories to you, my family and friends.

Chapter 10

Your Decisions Determine Your Destiny

"But if we hope for what we do not see, we
eagerly wait for it with perseverance."
Romans 8:25

The year 1974 was a weird and crazy year. People everywhere were still seething over the decision of the United States Postal Service raising the price of a "First Class" postage stamp to ten cents. People had actually protested in front of several of Charlotte's post offices. I remember one placard that read, "What's Next? Two Dimes?" That American crisis was then overshadowed by the headlines around the world acknowledging that India had test fired some kind of "atomic apparatus." However, even that historic event was soon dominated by the "impeachment hearings" and subsequent resignation of President Richard Nixon.

Despite all that was emerging in the world and national headlines, I was facing my own crisis. It was one of the darkest days of my young pastoral life. I just could not believe that my spiritual leaders over me would not accept what I was saying to them. I repeated it the third time to Dr. Glenn Burris, Sr., the supervisor over the Southeast District of Foursquare Churches.

"Brother Burris, he said that when he comes back, he will post the condemned sign at both doors of the church." He once again responded, and this time with more firmness, "Tim, they will not condemn a church." We were at a stalemate. What was I to do?

This started two days earlier with a gentle knock at the door of the parsonage, located next door to our old farmhouse church. "It has come to our attention that your church building does not meet the current zoning laws for 'public meeting'." My heartbeat was increasing as he continued. "You will not be able to continue meeting in your building until you are able to comply with the zoning ordinances. We have no record of your requesting or subsequent permit granted by the city, for you to use this eighty-year-old building for a public meeting place."

I nervously cleared my throat, "Sir, I have only been here for three years, but this has been a church since 1963." His response was quite clear, "Well, you are illegal."

The city official returned in seventy-two hours just as he had said he would do. We were standing outside the main entrance to our church sanctuary. He was leaning against the car that displayed the "City of Charlotte" insignia.

"Sir, I don't know what to do. I know that we have a lot of new families in our church and our small sanctuary is full. I know that people are parking in the grass because we don't really have much of a parking lot, but I have no other place to go." I continued with earnestness, "Sir, if you could just give us some time to try to deal with this. Please!"

He Responded, "How much time are you talking about?" I said, "If you could just give us one year to make the proper decisions." He dropped his head and was silent for what seemed a lifetime. "Reverend, I want you to step up to my car and look in the back seat."

I stepped forward and looked through the glass window.

Now after more than three decades since that major day in my life, I am still unable to clearly express the full emotion of my heart at that mind-boggling moment. It was emotion filled with disappointment, letdown, and worst of all, a sense of personal failure and defeat. The sign clearly said *"CONDEMNED, Foursquare Church, 6800 The Plaza."* I just stood there gazing through the glass. After several minutes of silence between us, the official soberly said, "I may lose my job over this decision, but I am going to leave. I will do my best to buy you thirty days, but believe me, Reverend, when I return, I will post both signs." All I could say was, "Thank you, sir!"

Both Claudia and I wept. We met with our growing church family, and they were all stunned! Several individuals had made phone calls on their own initiative and had confirmed what we were facing. We prayed earnestly asking God for both wisdom and mercy. The decisions we made would greatly change all of us.

Bob, who was one of our members and an architect, began drawing some basic plans for a new church building. We were able to sign an agreement with Joppa Masonic Lodge, several miles across town from us in order to use their facilities on Sunday mornings. We called the utility companies and requested that they come and disconnect and remove all electrical, telephone and water lines. We began dismantling windows, doors, toilets, sinks and some of the interior plywood paneling. We sold some of the items and gave away the rest.

It was a day that I will never forget. Henry, a contractor, had agreed to bring his bulldozer to the church site in order to demolish the building. The building had been gutted. All of the utilities had been disconnected. A host of our church members were present. Henry had pulled the bulldozer up to a key spot next to the building and then raised the long arm with a bucket claw, resting it on the corner of the roof. He then turned off the motor and climbed down from the dozer and made his way to where I was nervously standing.

"Preacher, are you sure that this is what we are supposed to do?" As I looked into his eyes I responded, "Henry, they are not going to condemn this church!" After that heartfelt and emotional reply, he then made his way back to the tractor and fired up the engine. That small building was old, so it didn't take long for Henry to bring it down, crumple it and shove it to the backside of our property.

"Preacher! Preacher!" It was the emotional voice of C.J., one of our newest members. He rushed over to where I was standing and shouted, "It took only twenty-six minutes for the church building to come down! Twenty-six minutes!" Perplexed, I just looked at him.

We, as a church family, had taken a huge step. We were in unity. We were determined to establish a church in the bustling city of Charlotte, North Carolina. We were praying for God's wisdom and mercy. God would not fail us, but it would not come easy. My first challenge was my supervisor. He was standing on the other side of the freshly graded ground.

I then made my way across the dirt where our church building had been standing just an hour before. My heart was pounding. Dr. Burris, Sr. was standing on the edge of the road that was at the front of our property with his hands on his hips. Pastor Dennis from a neighboring Foursquare Church in Gastonia was busy trekking across the property, taking pictures with his camera. It was a day that I will never forget.

My denomination was very concerned about my youthful

inexperience in such a scenario, and rightfully so. I was concerned, too. I had been in continual communication with the leaders over me about how the local government had made it very clear that our old farmhouse church building, sitting on the outskirts of this growing city, did not meet the standards for "public meeting" and was in the process of being condemned and closed down.

As I stood in front of Dr. Burris, Sr., what I remember most was his quivering upper lip. He said, "I assume that you have received permission from headquarters to tear down your church building?" My nervous response was, "No, sir."

"You understand that this church building belonged to the denomination," he strongly affirmed. "Dr. Burris, the denomination's church was condemned," I replied. With understandable agitation in his voice, he asked, "I assume that you have the money to rebuild another church?" "We only have about $5,000, which is only enough to pour the concrete slab," was my sobered reply. I apologized to him for the pressure that this was bringing on his office. "Dr. Burris, God called Claudia and I to the city of Charlotte, and we are determined not to disappoint Him."

The next morning was Sunday, and our church family gathered for church at the Joppa Masonic Lodge. Our two fire engine red buses had pulled up with a lot of new faces. Our old church building was gone. We were in our temporary location and now beginning a new season. I was exhausted but full of anticipation about our future.

I cannot recall what the theme of my Sunday morning message was, but I will never forget that day. "Preacher! Preacher!" shouted the familiar voice of C.J. "Praise God! Twenty-six people accepted Christ at the front! Didn't you count them? Twenty-six people!"

We had now advanced several weeks from that extraordinary weekend. The men in our church family, led by Bob and Darrel, had been digging and grading the site where our new church was to be built in preparation for the concrete floor. These guys had been taking turns with hand shovels and picks in digging the footers for the foundation. The men and women in our church had all been working feverishly.

Bob, the architect within our congregation, had drawn the plans for our 108' x 50' church. The new sanctuary would seat four hundred, along with a simple platform and beautiful baptistery. We would have a pastor's study along with five classrooms, a large nursery area with a sizable glass window looking directly into the rear of the sanctuary. The spacious foyer for the entrance from the new and expanded parking lot had us all smiling joyfully. However, how all of that was going to actually happen and be paid for had me very sobered.

As the second booming concrete truck was unloading the cement, my eyes caught Claudia waving her arms at me on the other side of the property. I made my way around the site to where she was standing to hear her say, "Honey, there's a lady on the telephone that wants to talk with you." I sighed out of frustration and then followed Claudia into the parsonage. That phone call was going to greatly impact our lives and ministry.

That gentle and nervous voice identified herself as Darrel's mother. She said, "Pastor Kelton, I understand that you are trying to build a new church. I want to help." I wasn't sure about what she meant. She continued, "It has been good for my son Darrel and his wife Mickie to come to your church." I responded,

"We're glad to have them. We're working Darrel pretty hard right now." Then came her amazing words, "Well, I want to loan you some money. I don't have a lot, but I just feel like this is what I'm supposed to do." My voice was now nervous when I responded, "How much money are you talking about?" She gently and timidly said, "Twenty thousand dollars." I was stunned to silence!

She then continued, "It's in my savings account at the bank. If you'll meet me, I can get the money to you today. It's a loan. I need you to pay me back, but I'm not in a hurry for it. I just want to help you get that new church building built."

I know it may seem foolish, but I hurriedly put on a tie and sport coat and made my way to her bank. We greeted each other with smiles and excitement. Someone could have easily thought that I was one of those con men hustling money from an older lady. Perspiration was trickling down my cheeks as I stood in the middle of the bank waiting for her.

She turned and walked over to me. She had this gentle and pleasant smile upon her face as she handed me the check for $20,000 made out to the First Foursquare Church.

"We need to have one of the bank officials help us draft a paper stating that you are loaning this money to us," I stated. She then pointed with her finger as I followed her out of the bank onto the sidewalk entryway. She then determinedly asked, "Pastor Kelton, can I trust you to pay me back?" My response was just as determined. "Ma'am, I promise you! You will get all of your money back plus interest." Then with a tone of rebuttal, she said, "I only want the twenty thousand dollars back. No interest! You don't charge God interest!" We both smiled.

Meanwhile, back at the church, the final delivery of concrete had been made. It was an overwhelming picture for this young pastor. As I soberly walked toward that bare and wet 5,400 square foot concrete slab, I was pondering the miracle of that twenty thousand dollar loan and wondering how many more miracles it would take to fill that empty concrete floor.

One of the next miracles that transpired was my fulfilling the twenty-one day fast that God had stirred within me. It was the longest fast without food that I had accomplished to that time in my life. Fasting has never been easy for me. Most people would probably say the same. However, I have never found any act of surrender in my personal life that equals the satisfaction and sense of accomplishment like that of fasting.

For a period of three weeks, while I was weaker in my physical body, I was growing in strength spiritually. I am sure that was the primary purpose of God stirring up the desire for a prolonged fast within me. As a pastor and spiritual leader in the midst of a growing church family along with the numerous obstacles that stood before me, determined prayer and fasting brought a tremendous strength to my daily life.

The miracle of that new church building gradually going up was one of the greatest joys of my life; however, as crazy as this may sound, there was a continued awareness within me that the success of the construction was daily linked to my fruitfulness in prayer and several other prolonged fasts during those critical months. There was no doubt within me as to our continued need for God's presence and leadership in this ongoing venture.

I was quickly learning as a young pastor that the devil was against most anything that I was for and would go to great lengths to not only hinder but defeat the objectives that lay before me. On a few occasions, some of my church family along with several of my fellow colleagues in the pastoral ministry accused me of being "too devil conscious." I responded to one of them with words of disappointment in their accusations, "I wish you were walking in my shoes, and then you would understand!"

For example, I just couldn't believe how much trouble we were having in launching our third bus into ministry. Granted it was another one of those older buses from the county school system, but it was running quite nicely until we pulled it up onto our church property. We were stunned when the crankshaft just fell to the parking lot gravel. The next day, two of the six tires were flat and the battery was dead. Of course some would say, "What did you expect from an old, worn out school bus that only cost you $600?"

Well, in time, we got Bus Number 3 coated with fire engine red paint along with those beautiful white doves painted on each side. It was now making its way into the heart of Charlotte with our committed leaders, as they would pick up dozens of children and youth and bring them to church, many of them accepting Jesus Christ into their tender hearts.

In time, that beautiful church building was completed with the cedar siding exterior walls along with the sharp looking hip roof. The glass was installed. The sheetrock was completed and painted. The lights overhead were placed into position. The central air conditioning and heating units were installed. The carpet was laid. The beautiful baptistery was placed just behind the platform. The classrooms were prepared for the children and youth. The beautiful nursery wall was painted with the scene of Noah and his animals making their way to the ark.

What an historic day it was when community and national leaders joined us for that dedication Sunday in 1975. Jim Bakker brought a heart-touching message. Dr. Nichols from Los Angeles led in the prayer of dedication. Claudia and I along with our church family tearfully and audibly thanked our heavenly Father for a new and beautiful place of worship. A new day had now dawned and none of us would ever be the same.

Chapter 11

HIS HANDS EXTENDED

"In all your ways acknowledge Him, and He shall direct your paths."
Proverbs 3:6

It was a late night telephone call that would have a significant impact upon my life and ministry. David Valesquez, leader of the Christian Latin singing group *The Amigos* was apologetic about the lateness of the call.

"Pastor Kelton, we are extending to you an invitation to join us for a week of ministry in Guatemala City." He then continued with an odd question, "Do you have a current U. S. Passport?"

My mind was quickly boggled with the thought of going to Guatemala, a nation that had been in the recent world and national headlines for several months. A devastating 7.5 killer earthquake had destroyed entire Guatemalan towns and villages with a rising death toll of over 22,000 of its citizens. I did finally reply to David, "Yes, I do have a current passport. My wife and I led a study tour to Israel and Rome two years ago. It is still a valid passport."

He immediately expressed excitement. David then said, "Pastor, we are scheduled for seven days of ministry in just a few weeks from now. We are a group of four singers but, none of us are preachers. We need you to travel with us and preach in several special meetings." He continued, "As you know, that nation is in desperate need of support, and we believe that God has called us to this mission." Then with an obvious hesitation in his voice, he said, "I need to tell you that we have already invited two other Charlotte pastors before calling you, but they both declined our invitation." It was humbling to hear that I was not their first or even their second choice.

I knew very little about these four young men, although I had seen them on the *PTL Club* and was impressed with their enthusiasm for Christ. There was little doubt that the need for ministry in the nation of Guatemala would be beneficial to the Kingdom of God. As it has been so many times in my life and ministry, I couldn't find the simple word "no." So, I began to immediately prepare myself. However, I truly had little understanding of what was before me and those very special and gifted young men.

It was a mixture of excitement and apprehension as we were landing at the airport outside of Guatemala City. We had been encouraging each other to remember that this mission that we were on was to bring encouragement to this nation, in spite of the horrendous damage done by the recent major earthquake as well as the tragic loss of human life. We were to be ambassadors of encouragement.

I can only tell you that the reports through the international media were unable to convey the stark reality of death and destruction in that nation. We were all stunned as we witnessed the mix of life that was pressing on in spite of the rubble of crushed buildings and mass burial sites. Housing, businesses, churches, schools, roadways and bridges were ravaged by this earthquake. As we stood gazing at a clock tower on one business building, we were reminded of the exact moment of that event.

The clock was frozen in time at 3 a.m. This unforgettable event had occurred on the morning of February 4, 1976. In spite of all that had happened before our arrival, here we were looking at a picture of ourselves along with a current article about our presence in this capitol city featured in the *Prensa Libre* newspaper, dated June 4, 1976.

Our primary ministry was taking place within a large, independent charismatic congregation called Prince of Peace Church, with senior pastor Munoz. The Sunday morning crowd of 2,000 was the largest group of people that I had ever stood in front of. I was so excited and yet so humbled as I stood nervously on that platform.

Again and again, I have been overwhelmed by the abundance of opportunities that God has opened to me, who in the eyes of some could see Tim Kelton as a *nobody*. With three generations of atheism on my father's side and generations of witchcraft on my mother's side of the family that preceded me, yet here I stood, in my first experience of bi-lingual preaching, hoping to influence a new generation towards faith in the God of the Bible. It would forever change my life.

That Sunday morning message was simply entitled, *The Prodigal Son,* as I related the powerful testimony of my older brother, David Kelton, pertaining to his sixteen years of addictions and amazing conversion to Christ. At the encouragement of the interpreter standing beside me, that message was interrupted with an emotional and joyful applause to God's grace and intervention on David's behalf.

That same evening, I chose to bring a message that I had been working on for several weeks in order to preach to my own congregation back in Charlotte, North Carolina. It was entitled,

The Power in Christ's Blood. I was deeply moved as I noted the emotional reaction of the young interpreter, Haroldo Contreras. At one moment during the message, he just stopped and tearfully looked at me as I was relating my recent studies pertaining to "blood." I discovered later that Haroldo was a medical student at one of Guatemala's colleges. He seemed to be stirred deeply at the study and comparison that "human life" is granted and sustained within our own blood, and "spiritual life" is granted through the sacrificial shed blood of Jesus Christ on the Cross. *"For the life of the flesh is in the blood, and I have given it to you upon the altar to make atonement for the soul"* (Leviticus 17:11).

As *The Amigos* stepped back to the platform following both messages that day, they were truly anointed in how they extended and invitation for those who desired Christ into their lives to make their way to that altar. Brothers David, Lorenzo and Chico Velasquez, along with drummer Ricardo Quintana, sang and played their musical instruments with deep and loving compassion on that platform. They were truly ambassadors of encouragement.

Pastor Munoz extended a loving invitation to us to remain for three additional days of ministry. We enthusiastically accepted. We were to continue with the same format of ministry. *The Amigos* would begin each service with a mini-concert in Christian music, and then I would be responsible for a message from my heart and the Bible. We were told that hundreds of hungry hearts accepted Christ during that historic ten days of ministry.

Upon our return to the United States, we were keenly aware that the experiences of those past ten days were a direct result of walking in obedience to God's call upon each of our lives. We could take very little credit for what we saw transpire during that mission journey. I know that I began learning a fundamental truth during that historic season of ministry. It has become more of a fabric of my being today, over three decades later, than when I first witnessed it. The truth that *timing is everything when following God!*

During the next year of 1977, I began a journey unlike anything that I had ever imagined pertaining to my life and ministry. It was late at night and I was sitting in our new sanctuary in an attitude of prayer. There were so many concerns upon my heart, and I just simply needed some time alone in prayer before God.

Somewhere in those several hours of prayer, I had maneuvered my way to the piano bench of that beautiful baby grand piano that had recently been given to our church as a gift. I found myself touching the keys and enjoying the sounds of the simple music that was coming forth. Don't misunderstand me; I am not a musician or pianist, but I can formulate some pleasant musical sounds like most anyone can by simply pushing down on the keys.

As I was humming some tunes, still in a prayerful attitude, I was stunned when I found myself singing audibly several words that eventually turned into sentences. I was aware that these sentences were thoughts that I did not want to lose. So, I hurried over to my office and got one of my note pads and quickly wrote down those sentences.

In the next few days I pulled some of our musically gifted members to that piano and asked them to listen to the few chords that I was playing along with the words that I had written down. It was a moment that I will never forget when those members congratulated me on writing a new song. I was absolutely stunned at their response but somehow understood what had actually transpired in my life.

Over the next several weeks and months, God inspired a number of songs and melodies deep in my heart. Those capable and gifted ladies—Diane, JoAnn and Nancy—helped to transcribe the music into its proper form. They encouraged me to copyright two of those songs for publication before 1977 ended. I was truly amazed at the continuing inspiration for writing music that stirred in my heart over the next several years.

Well, the year 1979 had just begun, and another historic season of ministry for Tim Kelton was upon the horizon. In less than three years from those 10 days of ministry in Guatemala in 1976, I would surrender to another invitation for ministry overseas. Once again, my life would be forever changed as a result of this twenty-one-day ministry journey to the Philippine Islands.

It was an extremely cold February morning when I boarded the jet at the Raleigh-Durham Airport in North Carolina. I would have an overnight stay at the Holiday Inn adjacent to the JFK International Airport in the chilly and snowy New York City. My departure for Manila, the capitol of the Philippines, was scheduled early the next morning.

It may seem comical, but I did not truly perceive just how long an overseas air journey to that part of the world would take. Yes, I had been told by the Pan American Airline representative that sold me the round trip ticket that the non-stop journey would take approximately twelve hours, but somehow that just didn't register properly in my brain. Do you know how long a twelve-hour, non-stop flight is?

You can eat a full meal, go to the restroom, read the entire thirty-one chapters of the book of Proverbs along with two complete Christian magazines; then go to the restroom again, look out the window for significant landmarks such as part of Alaska, according to the pilot; then take a two hour nap, awaking startled, praying for that poor mother to please calm that wacky four-year-old kid down; drink some soda pop and down two packages of specialty peanuts; then go to the restroom once again and discover you still have approximately six hours to go.

At that point I was thinking that I had made a serious mistake about this missions journey and was trying to figure out which one of those verses in Proverbs would identify Tim Kelton. You know, where Solomon was talking about a "fool."

Finally, the stewardess announced our arrival at the Narita International Air Port, just outside the metropolitan city of Tokyo, Japan. With a four-hour layover there while waiting for my flight to Manila, I enjoyed a long brisk walk around that brand new international terminal. It had just opened the year before. The two dozen or so jets that were parked around that huge complex were all 747 Jumbo's that seemed to be from every nation.

If there could be a highlight from a period of waiting four hours for your next flight, I definitely was blessed with it. As I had been making my way around the terminal I noticed a large delegation of reporters with flashing lights steadily moving through the corridor. Like many other folks in the terminal, I made my way closer so as to see what was going on. I was stunned when my eyes fell on the face of a famous singer and movie star. It was none other than Pat Boone. Like all the other crazies in that frenzied crowd, I, too, hurried over to see if I could shake his hand, and believe it or not, I was successful. As I quickly reached my hand toward him, he kindly responded by shaking my hand with a gentle smile. I then quickly said, "I'm a Foursquare pastor from North Carolina on my way to the Philippines for three weeks of ministry."

Believe this or not, he actually stopped and simply replied, "God bless you on your journey, pastor." He then headed on down the corridor. Yes, it's true, but I enjoyed it like an immature kid. I did take advantage of my knowledge that he and his family were members in the huge Foursquare Church in Van Nuys, California, pastored by Dr. Jack Hayford.

Well, I finally boarded my flight to Manila and was so grateful that I was now approaching a historic season of ministry for my life within the Philippine Islands, a nation located on more than 7,000 islands of which less than 1,000 of them are inhabited. The English language is widely spoken throughout that nation.

As I was making my way down the steps from the jet and on to the concrete walkway, I could not believe how hot it was. I was absolutely astounded. I complained to myself about the heat all the way through the terminal to the baggage area. By the time I got my suitcase and slowly worked my way through customs and then finally made it to the outside corridors, I had removed both my suit coat and matching vest as well as loosened my neck tie.

The folks that picked me up saw that I was sweating profusely and asked if I was okay. My simple response was, "I guess so." As we made our way to their car I asked, "How hot is it in Manila today?" Their smiling response was, "In the nineties as usual." I then explained to them that I had just come out of below freezing temperatures accompanied by snow flurries twenty-four hours earlier. Then their smiles quickly disappeared, and mine slightly reappeared.

The next morning I was en-route on a small Philippine airliner to the city of Davao. I would lodge in the home of the family that was in leadership over the Foursquare Churches within this region. They were so cheerful and accommodating, but they were concerned about a few potential problems that I might have. For instance, they explained that there was no "hot" water in the house. By that they meant that there was only a one-handle faucet in both the sink and tub in the bathroom, and that was because there was generally no need for hot water in the hot climate of the Philippines. There next concern, which they had already discerned the look upon my face, was the abundance of little "green geckos" all over the house. You know, like little green lizards. They explained how those little creatures were such a blessing, as they would help to eradicate their homes of the large quantity of flies and mosquitoes. They appealed to me to not be alarmed by them because they were harmless, friendly and like family.

However, one item that they forgot to warn me about was their "rooster" who was caged up just outside of my bedroom window. That wacky "rooster" was up and ready to go at 4 a.m. the next morning. I nearly jumped out of the bed from the laying position I was so shocked. If that wasn't enough as to my second morning in the Philippines, I then saw this little "green gecko" sitting on my chest just looking at me. My heart nearly stopped.

Over the next several days I did my best to become friendlier with the little guy, as I would continue to see him maneuvering around the bedroom, but I was still nervous. Of course it didn't help matters much on that weird morning that I nearly smashed him as I had almost put my right foot in my shoe as he barely escaped. By the way, I named him "Mr. Goggle Eyes."

For the next few days, I would be involved in nightly ministry within several of the area churches. Some of those churches were unable to understand English, so interpreters were necessary. However, that did not hinder those listeners. I was amazed at their intensity and determination to receive from this messenger. They were so hungry for spiritual food.

It was a remarkable afternoon as I was escorted to the *Thompson Christian School* in Davao. Those elementary-age school kids just went wild when I played a little basketball with some of them. They were all smiles and giggling when I then made the effort to shake each one of their hands, asking them to tell me there individual names. That took about an hour. My eyes were full of tears as I said goodbye and stopped for a group picture with many of them.

The next day I departed for Cebu City on another Philippine airliner, where I would spend a week teaching in the Bible College. What a discerning group of students and leaders they were. It became a daily event as to their desiring time to ask me questions that covered everything from my own personal life and ministry to them seeking my insight and thoughts as to global problems. I was amazed at their depth of maturity and concern for the world.

One of the most memorable moments in my life was when the Director of the Bible College approached me on my final evening there, asking if we could have a private time together. He then audibly reviewed my teaching on spiritual warfare that I had presented to the students and faculty.

He soberly stated, "I haven't even thought of some of the teaching that you have presented the last few days." Then with tears in his eyes as he proceeded to shake my hand, he said, "Thank you my brother, for coming from America and imparting your gift to us."

I was awakened early the next morning by the joyful voices and accompanying music of about a dozen of the students. They knew that I was scheduled to catch an early flight out of Cebu City, and they desired to serenade me as I departed. I had never been serenaded before. My face was a mix of smiles and tears as I hugged each of them and set out to the airport.

My next destination was Iloilo city. These two days of ministry had not been originally scheduled. The top leader in Manila had asked me if I would be willing to change my itinerary to include this island and town center that rarely had any outside visitors. I am so grateful that I consented. The impact of those two days of ministry upon my personal life was immense.

The primary leader for our denomination in Iloilo City was a gentle and discerning lady pastor. She had invited all the regional pastors and their leaders to join with her for two days of ministry with this thirty-one-year old pastor from Charlotte, North Carolina. Her church facility was absolutely packed. There were people standing outside of the sanctuary, leaning through the dozen or so open windows, and the temperature was very hot. I was continually sweating.

The message that was stirring in my heart was a mix of challenging those believers to stand strong against the devil and his numerous strategies to deceive them along with my heartfelt desire to challenge them to not only touch but change their world for the cause of Christ. One of my consistent Scripture readings was from the lips of Jesus: *All authority has been given to Me in heaven and on earth. Go therefore and make disciples of all nations, baptizing them in the name of the Father and of the Son and of the Holy Spirit, teaching them to observe all things that I have commanded you; and lo, I am with you always, even to the end of the age"* (Matthew 28:18–20).

With that opening session beginning mid-morning, I had preached my heart out for well over an hour and was thinking that it was time for a break. I had then closed with a simple prayer for God to continue to empower us to fulfill our tasks and sat down on one of the platform chairs. That sensitive and discerning pastor then made her way to the platform and leaned over to gently inquire, "Brother, is that all that you have to say?"

I sheepishly grinned at her as I responded, "Uh, no ma'am, I still have more to say." Then with a motion of her hand toward her small wooden pulpit, she said, "Brother, my pulpit, please speak to us until you are finished." I then stood up and walked back to the pulpit and picked up where I had left off.

It was an amazing time for me. I had not seen that kind of hunger and determined focus in search of Biblical truths before, at least not with that sense of intensity. Thankfully, she did make her way back to the platform and rescued me. After more than three hours, she announced that it was time for a break. She and her husband then led me outside to sit under one of the large shade trees adjacent to the church building. I was all smiles when she handed me two unopened Coca-Cola bottles. I discovered later that she had sent a couple of her church youth out in a small canoe to an anchored merchant ship in the nearby harbor. They had obtained those two bottles of soft drink especially for this guest preacher. I can only say that I had no idea that Coca-Cola tasted so wonderful.

Oh well, forget the so-called break from teaching. Most of the people that had been in the church sanctuary had now gathered outside and were encircling the huge shade tree where we were sitting and began asking for permission to ask me questions. When they were given the go-ahead, the questions began, covering everything from information about my wife and children and the church that I was pastoring, to my thoughts on Biblical prophecy and the end of the world.

I was one exhausted preacher as that pastor and her husband drove me to the airstrip the next day. My mind was boggled during the entire flight to Manila, where I would lead the final week of ministry in the Philippine Islands. You see, I clearly understood better than anyone that I was not some great preacher and expositor of the Bible; but the tearful parting words and goodbyes from that sincere pastor thanking me for not only touching her congregation but the numerous other spiritual leaders from that region so humbled me. Once again I knew that I owed the God of the Bible a debt that I could never repay.

My experiences in Manila and the region of Luzon were life changing. For one, I had never seen such a mesh and congestion of humanity before. I mean no disrespect to the citizens of Manila, but when it comes to driving a vehicle, they are "wacky." While automobile horns are important when needed to most of us, the drivers in that major city seemed to think that as long as the car is in forward gear, the horn is supposed to be honking; and that is as they hurriedly zip in and around each other.

I had never seen a massive four-way traffic jam before my arrival in Manila. I am not exaggerating when I say there could not have been less than one hundred cars, stagnated bumper to bumper, at an intersection with traffic lights. Passengers in the cars then got out and asked other drivers to please back up so traffic could get through. With amazing finesse and due diligence, in the space of about ten or fifteen minutes, the traffic would once again be flowing. That is until the next major traffic jam would build up.

I was very nervous about making an extensive trip to Muntinlupa City by myself. It would be my first time in a crowded public bus while there. I will never forget the small wooden crate with several noisy chickens sitting in the aisle of the bus. Several other passengers had large bags full of various vegetables that they were traveling with.

I was shocked to discover that the bus would not take me the whole distance. No one had told me that. I anxiously hailed a taxi, or what the Philipinos call a "jeepney." Thankfully I did have a pocket full of Philippine Pesos. Not fully understanding the words of that driver, I thought that this vehicle would get me to my desired location, but once again I was wrong.

Stunned would not have clearly described my frame of mind when I discovered that it was now necessary for me to climb on the back of a small motorcycle for the final leg of this journey. I would have to pay this driver two pesos to finally get me to the *New Bilibid Prison.*

For me to have this opportunity for ministry was both challenging and rewarding. I had been asked to spend my only free and unscheduled day at this Philippine federal prison. I had read that there were more than twelve thousand prisoners confined in this medium and maximum security prison. It was to be my great privilege to meet Olga Robertson, the primary chaplain for the prison. She was small in physical stature but large in her faith and Christian commitment to these thousands of prisoners. They called her "Mommy."

She had scheduled me to join her in several chapel-type gatherings within the maximum security section of the prison.

Those particular prisoners were not allowed to leave their general lock up area for such an event. She had heard that I was willing to openly share the testimony of my brother David and his conversion to Christ. So that was her primary request of me for those chapel gatherings.

I still have color photos of those prisoners dressed in bright orange uniforms sitting before me. Their bunk beds were lined up behind where they were sitting. I will never forget how surprised I was when I realized that there was a dead body laying on one of the top bunks only fifty feet from where we were. The guards would remove that covered body as soon as we had completed our set time within that particular unit.

Those prisoners were listening intently, especially each time I portrayed David's attempts to take his own life. Some even wiped away tears when I would describe a praying and weeping mother that refused to give him up to the devils deadly schemes. Many of their hands would be raised when I would ask for that signal of their desire to ask Christ into their hearts. I was not allowed to physically touch any of them for prayer or any other reason, and the four armed guards that escorted us made sure to remind us of that policy on several occasions.

After those six chapel gatherings, Olga asked me to follow her to the small church on the prison grounds. She had a very small apartment room within that church building. She wanted to talk with me and she wanted me to join her for lunch. As she prepared the rice and vegetables, she emotionally described the ongoing daily struggle that she lived with. She was in a lot of emotional pain over the recent execution of one of the inmates that she had led to the Lord and had been discipling for several months while he was on death row. Before I left that afternoon she asked the guards for permission to take me inside the execution room where the electric chair was. She then asked the guards for permission to take me out into the prison cemetery where this young man had been buried. As we stood at that graveside, she openly wept. I was to never be the same after that single day at the *New Bilibid Federal Prison*.

My final four days in Manila was just as life-changing. The Calvary Foursquare Church, situated in the heart of that bustling city, was the site for this special conference. I was humbled once again as I stood to that pulpit hoping to touch hundreds of those members who would come daily. They were hungry and searching for more of God. What a privilege it was to challenge those Philippine believers to go to other parts of the world and preach the Gospel. They were very sobered and quiet as I confronted them with the Scriptures and the reality that the "call to missions" was not just for Americans and Europeans. I was so thankful to be able to pray over a number of those believers as they made their way to the altar at the front of that beautiful sanctuary and surrendered their individual lives to God's will.

I was a weary preacher as I climbed on board that jumbo jet for my lengthy return trip back to the United States and my home town of Charlotte, North Carolina. However, those twenty one days in the Philippine Islands would forever change my perspective on the world.

The year 1979 would end up being one of the most significant years of my life pertaining to the ministry. As I was only a few days away from a second mission's journey during that year, the world and national headlines were full of the news pertaining to the recent assassination of South Koreas president, Park Chung Hee, on October 26. Those headlines were of particular interest to me because South Korea was where I was headed, and that was in just a few days.

After several months of correspondence and prayer with Ron and Charlotte, the missionary leaders from our denomination over South Korea, I was scheduled for sixteen days of ministry there in the first few weeks of November. A number of our local church members expressed their desire for me to cancel this scheduled trip, or at least delay it until 1980 because of their concerns for me during this unpredictable time in that part of Asia. However, after lots of prayerful consideration, the final decision was to press on.

After another lengthy flight from New York City to Tokyo, I was facing an additional challenge while I was delayed for two days in Japan. Because of the political instability in South Korea at that time, I was being required to update my visa for entrance there. That would require me to catch a taxi into the heart of the city of Tokyo, and then make my way to the South Korean Embassy. They were requiring any non-citizen of South Korea to re-register for entrance into their nation. They said it was a safety precaution, a result of President Park's assassination.

With that brief venture a success, I was now landing at the international airport in the capitol city of Seoul, one of the most populous cities in the world. I was surprised to discover that nearly half of all of South Korea's citizens live within the metropolitan region of Seoul. That bustling city of millions is located only thirty miles from the DMZ, demilitarized zone, the often volatile border that is shared with Communist North Korea.

It was an honor to enjoy fellowship with Ron, Charlotte and their children. They were a very gifted and respected couple and had been serving in South Korea for a number of years. Their home was located in the city of Taejon, several hours from Seoul.

November in South Korea was chilly just like it was in North Carolina when I departed for this journey. I was surprised that Ron asked me to hop on the back of his motorcycle with him in that cold air, but he was trying to take advantage of a few hours that we had so I could shop for some souvenirs for my family.

For nearly a week I would be privileged to teach at the *Daesung Christian High School,* located within the city of Taejon. This was a school of several thousand students. I was given the opportunity to teach on the subject of the life of Christ in numerous and separate grade level assemblies. However, I would also be required to conclude those assemblies with an opportunity for the students to have a question and answer session with me as well.

What was so significant about this unique time of ministry was the possibility to influence hundreds of those students who had come from Buddhist backgrounds. One of the leaders of that high school had told me that many of the students were practicing Buddhist's and yet were enrolled in this influential Christian high school.

I was awestruck at the daily response of so many of those sincere and energetic students. They displayed a definite hunger for more understanding as to the teachings of the Bible. They were full of questions about America, too. Many of them asked if they could practice their English on me. They were not timid and challenged me to correct them if they were in error.

Another inspiring moment for me was the opportunity to teach the college students that had enrolled in the small Christian Bible School in Taejon. They were endeavoring to prepare themselves to become future ministry leaders. Once again, I was personally inspired as those young people displayed a genuine determination to follow God's plan for their individual lives.

The privilege of standing in the pulpit of the Taejon Foursquare Gospel Church was immense for me personally. This was the central and headquarters church for that region. I was honored on both occasions to have the senior pastor stand beside me as the interpreter. Pastor Seen Ok Ahn touched my life so deeply at the end of that final sermon with a tearful request for my sermon notes. No one had ever made such a request of me before. I quickly responded by handing over those hand written notes on the subject of *"the foolishness of God."*

Before my departure back to the United States, I was offered an opportunity for ministry to Christian prisoners being held in the federal prison located in Seoul. It was not a large number of men, but most of them were being held for "crimes against the government." They were former communist North Koreans who at one time in their lives had plotted some kind of strategy against the South Korean government.

With several armed guards positioned around that meeting room, we were all seated as I endeavored to share with them the story of my brother David, and his miraculous deliverance from the chains of spiritual bondage that he had lived with for nearly two decades. Several of those political prisoners displayed their tearful emotions as I did my best to articulate that Jesus Christ was the only hope that any of us had.

As I was now on another lengthy flight back to America, my heart was full of gratitude to not only the spiritual leaders in South Korea, but to my Heavenly Father who had made this second mission journey in 1979 possible for me. I did not fully understand at that particular moment, but did somehow sense, that the day would come when I myself would be serving the Lord and His people full time on foreign soil.

Chapter 12

WHAT WOULD JESUS DO?

"Go into all the world and preach the gospel to every creature."
Mark 16:15

My heart was literally breaking as I listened to Claudia's continued weeping. She had collapsed on the adjacent bed in the room as I listlessly just laid there staring at the ceiling with a steady stream of tears trickling down my cheeks. It was the day in the spring of 1981 that we had been anxiously and joyfully awaiting, and yet look at us, lying on two separate beds in the Radisson Plaza Hotel in downtown Charlotte, crying.

We had resigned our eleven-year pastoral assignment in Charlotte just six months prior to this significant day. I had been asked to join with Dr. Glenn Burris, Sr., the Southeastern District Supervisor of our denomination, and serve as the Coordinator for the International Foursquare Convention to be held at the Charlotte Civic Center. We had also made application to our Missions Headquarters hoping to be considered for appointment as missionaries in Europe. Our primary desire and vision was to serve the Lord in London, England. One other major factor in all of this was that Claudia was six months pregnant.

One might wonder just why Tim and Claudia Kelton are laying in two separate hotel beds crying. After all, we had seen a fruitful season in our first pastoral assignment. We had been placed in a high profile position as "Convention Coordinator" and the convention was now in full motion. We had been selected for prayerful consideration to serve as missionaries, and we were excitedly awaiting the birth of our third child.

Well, just a few hours earlier, we had met with Dr. Leland Edwards, Director of Foursquare Missions. He had invited us to meet with him for lunch at a small café within the Radisson Hotel Civic Center complex and talk with him about a potential missionary assignment. Our hearts were racing with nervous anticipation as we sat down with him.

With distinct apprehension, he then began to dialogue with us about the process of selection for missionary personnel. Claudia and I were both smiling as he clearly stated that we had actually been chosen for appointment from a list of numerous applicants.

"Tim and Claudia, I know that you specifically stated in your application that your number one choice for appointment would be London." He continued, "However, we need you in another region of the world."

My heart had ceased racing and was now pounding. After seeing the troubled expressions upon both of our faces, he slowly and nervously said, "We would like to send you to the South Pacific, specifically, the Island of Papua New Guinea."

I am certain that my heart actually stopped. I remember trying to think, but my brain was not functioning right, but I do remember asking myself, "Did he say Papua New Guinea?" I then glanced at my beautiful bride of twelve years, and saw the tears welling up in her eyes.

Before either one of us could muster up a reply, Dr. Edwards gently but firmly said, "I need your decision by noon tomorrow." He then continued, "Tim, as you know, tomorrow night has been slated as "Missions Night," and I would like to call you and Claudia up to the platform to announce your appointment." I then said, "Dr. Edwards, why Papua New Guinea?" Without a moment of hesitation he stated, "We are in desperate need of your pastoral gift on that island." He then continued to dialogue with us over the next hour with more in depth details.

Well, you would think that the most memorable moment during that eventful week of convention for me personally would have been when I escorted friends like Jim and Tammy Bakker into the Civic Center Complex as invited guest ministers to the convention delegates. Or the extraordinary night that I was asked to escort renowned evangelist Jimmy Swaggert to the platform for an unforgettable night of music and ministry to the convention body. Or what about the night that Tim and Claudia Kelton stood front and center beside Dr. Edwards receiving the intense prayers of the convention body as newly appointed missionaries to Papua New Guinea.

No, it was none of those. The most memorable moment was Claudia and I embracing each other after several hours of weeping and searching of our individual hearts in order to be capable of surrendering our lives to the will of God for such an assignment. It was crystal clear that this would be a life-changing decision for Claudia and me, our three children, our families and our friends. In short order it would be confirmed to us through manifold circumstances that our lives would never be the same from that historic day forward.

Convention was over and we were now in a waiting mode, waiting for our baby to arrive. In the meantime we were busy making preparations for moving to a jungle island nearly ten thousand miles away from Charlotte, North Carolina. We were filing for passports and visas and making appointments with doctors for the needed inoculations. We were also packing clothing, bedding, medicines, toiletries, toys, books and our baby bed and high chair into twenty-one steel barrels and two wooden crates for three children who would each significantly change and grow over the next five years of our slotted appointment to Papua New Guinea.

I was personally startled to receive communications airmailed from Papua New Guinea from an old friend, Pastor Phil, my former youth pastor when I was a teenager. Remember he's the one that helped get us both in trouble at the Shoney's restaurant in Charlotte when we started throwing ice cream from our banana splits at each other. Now fifteen years later, he had been appointed as the interim "Field Director" following the outgoing pioneer missionaries in Papua New Guinea for our denomination, Mason and Virgene Hughes, who had served twenty-three years there. Phil Starr and his wife Millie were anxiously awaiting our arrival in the fall of 1981.

Those months of waiting had been very difficult. Our families had been communicating their concerns and personal struggles with releasing us to such a distant place as Papua New Guinea. I don't know that any foreign field would have been any easier as to their worries, but the thought of us living in a mostly jungle nation truly frightened most of our family members.

It certainly didn't help matters when the word slowly leaked out that we had not only received one letter from the U.S. State Department requesting that we reconsider our decision, but that the second letter was more sobering as it came as a "WARNING," advising us that the Papua New Guinean Government was an unstable government with an unsafe environment, as well as the serious words declaring the lack of medical healthcare available within that nation, especially when considering that we were taking three small children with us. Yes, those letters from the State Department were very troubling.

I had purchased a host of books containing information pertaining to the history of Papua New Guinea as well as the current conditions on that island nation. It was very sobering and foreboding. Both Claudia and I lost a lot of sleep at nights as we would prayerfully try to encourage each other to keep our eyes focused on the Lord and His call upon both of our lives.

I admit that my greatest moment of discouragement was when Angela, our seven-year-old, had traveled with me to the Southeast District youth camp in order to have a short visit with one of our denomination's veteran missionaries. *Camp Courtney,* located in Hendersonville, North Carolina, had become a very special place for our family. We had enjoyed many weeks at this camp over our eleven years of pastoring in Charlotte.

Dr. Edgar Coombs, missionary to South Africa, was one of the featured speakers during this particular summer camp season. I was privileged to have an afternoon with him, hoping to gain a better understanding of what I was to face in just a few months; however, the opposite occurred. I remember that afternoon like it was just yesterday.

We were sitting together on one of the benches overlooking the ball field and swimming pool. As we engaged in very heartfelt conversation as to the call of God upon both of our lives, he leaned over toward me and said, "Tim, I think you are making a mistake."

My mouth just dropped open. I was stunned at his statement.

"Dr. Coombs, what do you mean," was my emotional reply. He then firmly and soberly stated, "Tim, you are too old."

At that point, I felt completely defeated. This man was a highly honored and seasoned missionary with decades of experience on foreign soil, and he was telling me that I was about to make a mistake because I was too old. My mind was boggled.

"Dr. Coombs, my whole life I have been told that I was 'too young'—that some day, when I 'grow up' and 'mature,' that God will be able to use me." I tearfully continued, "Now today, at age thirty-three, you're telling me that I am 'too old.' I don't understand, sir."

He then reached over and patted my hand. "You don't know how demanding your assignment to Papua New Guinea will be upon you. It will require you to be away from your small children that will need you." He then crossed his legs and looked out toward the ball field and said, "You are too old to learn a new language. If you were ten years younger and without a family, you would then be much more capable of fulfilling this assignment as a missionary."

He gently continued, "However, I am proud of you. Not very many would position themselves such as you have. I am not here to discourage you, but to challenge you to keep your eyes focused on the Lord, especially if you maintain your present course." He then reached over and took my hand and prayed for God's protection and continued leadership in my life.

That evening as Angela and I headed back to Charlotte, my mind rehearsed that afternoon with Dr. Coombs, over and over. His words and prayer greatly impacted my life.

I can only tell you how deeply I was grieved when, years later, the news spread throughout our denomination that Dr. Edgar

Coombs was killed while still serving his Lord in the nation of South Africa. He had been in the process of simply changing a tire on his vehicle when he was struck by another moving automobile. It was our great loss, and heaven's gain.

Well, the day that we had been waiting for had finally come. Our son, Jonathan Paul, was born on July 7, 1981. In just nine weeks, we would step on to the soil of that South Pacific Island called Papua New Guinea.

Claudia's parents, Claude and Mary Fannin, had made their way from their home in New Castle, Indiana, to Charlotte. They along with my mother had been a tremendous help during this season of sorting and packing in preparation for our move overseas.

However, our most desperate situation was getting a picture of this newborn baby to accompany the application for his individual passport. The State Department had made it very clear to us that the process would take sixty days. I had been successful in obtaining the U.S. Passports and other proper documentation needed for myself, Claudia, Angela and Valerie.

Claudia was still too weak to go with me, so I asked Granny Mary to accompany me and ten-day-old baby Jonathan to the professional photographer. It was one of those historic events that will forever be burned on my brain.

The photographer was actually sweating as he had the lighting set just right along with his professional camera secured to a tripod stand. Jonathan was propped up in his small baby carrier beneath the lights with small blankets. The only problem that we were having was to get this ten-day-old baby to cooperate. The photographer had already taken at least a dozen snap shots, but none of them with Jonathan's eyes open. The State Department will not accept a photo for a passport unless the eyes are open. Granny Mary and I along with the nervous photographer kept softly poking his cheeks, gently touching his eyebrows and even delicately stroking his little lips in hopes that one of those maneuvers would actually get his two eyes to open for at least a second or two, but nothing was working.

Then it happened. The photographer asked us to prepare ourselves for his final ploy and to please cooperate with him. With his camera ready, the lighting set perfectly and Granny Mary and I cautiously sitting right next to the baby, the photographer asked me to loudly and briskly clap my hands just out of photo range. With a deep breath and flexed muscles, I obeyed his command. At the sound of the loud and forceful smack of my hands, both of Jonathan's eyes instantly popped open. The photo was snapped. The photographer's plan had worked.

The major problem we now had was this screaming ten-day-old infant in our midst. Baby Jonathan was wailing and shaking as I reached my hands into the baby carrier and picked him up. I was audibly trying to calm him down, but it wasn't working. I then handed him over to Granny Mary, who took him into her arms as she, too, attempted to rock him back and forth. She then handed him back to me as he was still wailing, and she was now crying. It took another ten minutes or so as I paced back and forth across the photography studio holding him against my chest and patting his bottom while audibly apologizing to my little son for nearly scaring him to death with the thunderous clap of my hands and yelp of my voice. All the way back home, Granny Mary kept saying to me, "We've ruined the poor little guy."

After grueling weeks of packing, emotional days of saying goodbye to family and friends in both North Carolina and Indiana, a week of final briefing at our Foursquare Missions Headquarters in Los Angeles, and a three-hour flight to Hawaii with a short twelve-hour overnight in Honolulu, we were finally on the last leg of our journey to Papua New Guinea. We had boarded an Air Nuigini Jet and flown out of the International Airport in Honolulu. This non-stop flight would take nearly nine hours before we would land at Port Moresby, the capitol of Papua New Guinea. We were very excited, and we were very nervous.

Papua New Guinea occupies the eastern half of the second largest island on earth. It is 400 miles wide and 1,500 miles long. Located near the equator, Papua New Guinea has towering jagged mountains, some of which are covered with perpetual snow, and also rugged jungle valleys, some containing boiling lakes and geysers. Fast moving rivers and giant rain forests are scattered across the landscape of the island. Earthquakes and trimmers are often felt. With a population of only four million people and yet more than seven hundred different dialects spoken, Papua New Guinea is considered one of the most challenging nations on earth.

From the moment our feet touched the ground in Port Moresby, our challenges began. After dragging our eight suitcases from the "International Zone," I would have to make sure they got to the loading area for the local air traffic, but I first had to get us through the customs section. Claudia and the kids had seated themselves near where I was standing. The equatorial heat was stifling. The customs officer then began opening each suitcase and carefully inspected each item. I was getting nervous as to how slow he was moving as I kept watching the clock nervously, understanding that we had to get those suitcases across the terminal so they could be loaded on another airplane for our flight to Goroka, our final destination. We didn't have much time before that flight took off, and I was feeling the pressure. There would not be another flight to Goroka for several days. I reminded the customs officer several times about our flight, and he would simply smile at me and say, "Everything will be okay."

Finally, he approved everything in our suitcases but several boxes of Gerber's Baby Food. He pointed at the picture of the banana on the exterior of the box and kept shaking his head in the negative. I tried to explain to him that there were no actual bananas in the box but he just kept shaking his head in the negative. I finally opened one of the boxes and poured the cereal flakes out into my hand hoping to show him that there were no actual bananas in that box, but he kept pointing at that picture of a banana and shaking his head in the negative. He finally confiscated all but one of the boxes, the only box that didn't have a picture of a banana on it. He then stamped all of our passports and said, "Welcome to Papua New Guinea."

He did telephone the tower and stopped our flight from leaving because we were late. We hurriedly rushed across the terminal, while they rushed our luggage out to load it. We then rushed to board the small fifty-passenger jet that was nearly full. In forty-five minutes we were landing on the airstrip at Goroka, located a mile high in the interior of that jungle island. This town center was to become our new home.

At the top of that mountain range the heat was much more bearable, but the odor was so difficult to get use to. As we were making our way off of that Air Nuigini Jet and down the mobile staircase, we could hear cheers. It brought smiles to all of our faces when we saw several signs waving in the air that stated, "Welcome! Kelton Family!"

I was quick to embrace my long time friend Phil Starr. He then began introducing us to several missionaries as well as national leaders. They were all smiles and were truly rejoicing at our arrival. It was a moment that we will never forget. Of course our two beautiful girls were an instant hit as well as our nine-week-old son. They helped us retrieve our suitcases, and then we headed to our new house located only a mile from the airstrip.

I had alerted Phil that this day of our arrival, September 13, would be Angela's eighth birthday. So, as part of their welcoming us to our new home with refreshments, they had also prepared a birthday cake. Everyone clapped their hands as we sang "Happy Birthday" to Angela.

I was truly overwhelmed when a young couple cornered me and joyfully introduced themselves. "Brother, we were so excited to learn that you would be our new leader here." As I timidly looked into their eyes, they continued, "Do you remember when you were preaching at the Calvary Foursquare Church in Manila several years ago?" "Of course I do," I quickly responded. "Well, we were both there during those special meetings," they cheerfully stated.

I was stunned and asked them to tell me more. "Your final message in that last service changed our lives. Do you remember?" asked Monsito. "Yes I do," was my response.

"We were not married at that time, but God brought us together. We each felt the call of God upon our lives that day, and we surrendered to his will as you had prayed," Monsito tearfully stated.

I instantly remembered that very church service. I had stated to that congregation of Philippino's that it was time for them to stop expecting missionaries to come from other lands to their nation and it was time for them to go to other nations and preach the Gospel. I remember that my sense was that message was not well-received. The silence across that large sanctuary was what some jokingly call "deafening." While there was a handful that had come forward for prayer, I felt that I had been to firm and actually regretted my final message in the Philippines.

However, today, my first day in Papua New Guinea, meeting this young couple named Monsito and Jojo was a most rewarding moment. We tearfully embraced each other and rejoiced over the reality that we would now be able to work together on this jungle island.

As the sun set on our first evening in this new land, we were all exhausted. We tucked the girls in for the night and had our nine-week-old baby son bundled up next to us. Claudia and I then prayerfully renewed our lives to God as we tearfully and emotionally dropped off to sleep.

Chapter 13

BE STRONG IN THE LORD

"You therefore, my son, be strong in the grace that is in Christ Jesus.
And the things that you have heard from me
among many witnesses, commit these to
faithful men who will be able to teach others also."
2 Timothy 2:1,2

This was our first sunrise in Papua New Guinea. I was recounting in my mind the many objectives that were before me over the next few days. One of those would be joining with Phil Starr, the interim Field Director, for a flight to the coastal town of Madang. He had set up a very rigorous and aggressive schedule for us over the next couple of weeks in order to introduce me to as many missionary personnel and national leaders across the nation as possible before the upcoming 25th Anniversary Convention and his departure back to the United States.

Angela, Valerie and I were having our first breakfast in Papua New Guinea at our kitchen table. Claudia was nursing Jonathan in the adjacent living room area. We were all excitedly and yet nervously gazing out the many windows in our new home, talking about all of the new sights and sounds around us.

The brown-skinned Papua New Guineans were streaming down the streets directly in front of our corner lot. The mothers were carrying their infants in special woven backpacks called "bilums" as well as balancing various kinds of bundles upon their heads. We were to quickly learn that these crowds of people would do this most every morning and afternoon as they would make their way to the busy outdoor market place and then head back to their homes and villages. Claudia and the children would soon join them at the market place on a regular basis.

With the growing sense of being overwhelmed with all that I was feeling, I excused myself from the family and headed to our bedroom. After slowly shutting the door, I pulled back the curtains from the windows overlooking that busy and noisy street in front of our house. I then sat down on the edge of our bed and stared out those windows. The equatorial heat was already working its way through the glass. I could not hold back the steady stream of tears.

"God, what have I done," kept going through my mind? "Here we are, ten thousand miles away from home. My precious and delicate daughters are uprooted from their family and friends. My beautiful bride and nine-week-old infant son are in such fragile condition." These thoughts just kept going over and over deep within my spirit. Remembering that staggering moment like it was just yesterday, I then said out loud, "God, please forgive me. I am not man enough to do this. I'm sorry."

A heartbreaking sense of shame then flooded me. With my elbows on my knees and my hands cupped around my face, I cried all the more.

It's not a new phrase, I have spoken it before; but today, several decades later from that sobering moment in my life, I can say it once again, *I owe God, the God of the Bible, a debt that I will never be able to repay.*

I never cease to be amazed at how the Holy Spirit is able

to touch the inner most parts of our lives, the deepest regions of our souls, even those areas within us that are the darkest and most hopeless. That September 14, 1981 morning in Papua New Guinea, was a moment of a rekindling of the call of God upon my life coupled with a renewed surrender to God's will that I had never sensed or witnessed before. I would never be the same.

My mind raced back six months to that small, elegant café in the Radisson Hotel Civic Center complex in downtown Charlotte where Claudia and I had met with Dr. Leland Edwards. I was remembering that heart-to-heart exchange about us receiving a missionary appointment from our Foursquare Denomination and my earnest question, "Dr. Edwards, why Papua New Guinea?" This day, once again, his quick and sincere response, "We are in desperate need of your pastoral gift," was pulsating through my heart and mind.

Believe me, I understood better than anyone that I was not this superb and successful pastor that should be seen as a picture of great achievement and accomplishment. I had not been sent to this far away island in the south pacific as some trophy deserving high accolades for the denomination that had sent me. Dr. Edwards had communicated a very clear picture to Claudia and me of where this island nation was now standing in need.

Mason and Virgene Hughes had laid a strong foundation in the twenty-three years that they had served on that island. Dr. Hughes was a gifted evangelist. He had traveled from one valley to another, from one town center to another, winning the hearts of thousands who had never heard the Gospel of Jesus Christ. In his fervor and enthusiasm for the Kingdom of God, he had planted and established over one hundred churches throughout that island.

However, the time had now come for "new leadership," and that did not mean "new missionary leadership." The Papua New Guinean National Church must now begin to take the leadership over their own destiny. Somehow, we had to find successful ways to pass the torch. It was to be Tim and Claudia Kelton's tremendous privilege to help begin that season of transition, but as you would only expect, that transition would not come easy or without cost.

As the new Field Director, I had been asked to close out the 25th Anniversary Convention with a final challenging message to the three thousand-plus Papua New Guineans and missionary personnel that were present. This would be their first time to hear their new leader speak, and of course they were hoping that they could approve of the denomination's appointment of this new, young thirty-three-year-old from America.

Before I stepped to the pulpit in that large gathering center, I had already come under siege. Just a few days earlier, the local New Zealand doctor had soberly communicated the results of the blood work that he had done on me. "You have all the elements of malaria at work in your body," he said, "and I am very concerned about the type of malaria that is signaling in the test results." Malaria was then and still is today a major health issue in Papua New Guinea. The Papua New Guinean's live with malaria within their systems but are somehow mostly immune to it. However, when those small, zebra-striped mosquitoes would bite them and then in time bite one of us expatriates, we would be in trouble. He pressed me on whether or not I had been faithful in taking my weekly dose of "anti-malarial" medication. I told him that I had not missed one dose, but nevertheless, I was extremely weak and struggling greatly.

To make things worse, our four-month-old baby, Jonathan, had become very sick as well. He was losing weight at a frightening pace. The doctor was scratching his head as to our son's illness, but kept encouraging us to keep fluids flowing into him.

That convention body had already fervently prayed for Jonathan and I before I began my short message. I thanked them for their prayers from the bottom of my heart and then asked them to listen to the simple but powerful words from the Old Testament Prophet Zechariah.

"This is the word of the Lord to Zerubbabel: 'Not by might nor by power, but by My Spirit,' says the Lord of hosts" (Zechariah 4:6).

I went on to briefly say that the future stability and accomplishments of the Papua New Guinean church would not be secured or strengthened through the might and power of men, but rather that future church would touch its own nation and other parts of the world through the power and might of the *Holy Spirit of God.*

I was embarrassed that I had run out of physical strength at that point, but I turned and just simply sat back down in a chair on the platform anyway. However, as one of the other leaders stepped up to where I had been standing, I was greatly encouraged when I personally witnessed hundreds of those Papua New Guinean leaders raise their hands to demonstrate their commitment to touching their villages, towns, communities, nation and their world for the cause of Jesus Christ in those closing minutes of that historic 25th Anniversary Convention week. The "passing of the torch" had now begun.

Several months later, in our very first gathering of key leaders from within our denomination from across the island, I informed them that they were now in charge of their leadership and decision-making meetings. I confirmed to them that I would maintain one vote on voting matters, and would be willing and ready to offer my advice and counsel when called upon, but "the torch" that required deep spiritual thought and Biblical wisdom as to their future was being handed to them. I reminded them regularly that the God of the Bible would hold them responsible for their decisions.

Please understand that I certainly had not taken a back seat. I was still very much on the front line as I traveled from village to village and town to town endeavoring to "pass the torch."

One of our leaders had introduced me to a deacon in a village that I had traveled to. He explained to me that this particular man currently had four wives and desired to marry a fifth wife, but the leaders were hesitant to bless the marriage. They wanted my opinion to be publicly stated within that village.

As I have previously stated numerous times, I am so grateful for the leadership of the Holy Spirit. I know this looked and sounded strange, but it is what I instantly sensed that I should do. I reached out my hands and arms and wrapped them around this small man in stature and pulled him close to me. Without any resistance from him whatsoever, he laid his cheek against my chest. I then gently spoke to him through the interpreter that had traveled with me, "No more wives." I then prayed that he would devote the rest of his life to loving and caring for the family that he now had. As we gently separated from each other, I was relieved that he presented a smile as he patted my hands and thanked me for giving him wisdom.

I had flown by small aircraft into a more remote region because I had heard that men from another village had burned down one of our Foursquare churches. Many of our Foursquare members were angry and were actually preparing for what is a very common practice in Papua New Guinea called "pay back." My appeal to our Foursquare brethren in that remote village was reciting to them the teaching of Jesus as to forgiving those who have hurt us by a total of four hundred and ninety times. I then quickly started counting out loud while extending my fingers with each number hoping to visually demonstrate to them just how many four hundred and ninety times was. Then one of the village men walked over to me and tearfully responded that he clearly understood the point that I was making. The interpreter then shared with me the villager's conversations as they prayerfully decided against retaliation. In time, peace actually prevailed between those two villages.

Several of our key leaders had asked me to join them for another flight into a remote region by the sea. As I sat with our men and listened to their dialogue with a number of leaders in this large village, and as the picture became more and more clear, I became pretty somber. When our men turned and asked me for my opinion and leadership in this particular matter, I responded, "The Gospel of Jesus Christ is not for sale. If this village welcomes the Foursquare Church, we will do everything that we can to help the village, but we cannot promise them possessions and goods and services as a part of a competitive bid for a presence in the community."

Our men then joined together for a few minutes of prayer together and then returned to dialogue with these village fathers. There was a cordial and friendly goodbye as we then made our way back down the long trail to the grassy airstrip. We discovered later that another denomination had been permitted to build a church within that village, based upon numerous promises of gifts, goods and services that would be provided by that denomination to the village.

I shouldn't have been surprised at the abundance of opportunities that would continually arise providing ample opportunity to teach those discerning national leaders principles in Christian living and meaningful ministry to their world. I made every effort to never travel and minister alone for the single purpose of teaching by example.

Several of us had traveled to a village that was earnestly seeking encouragement. The young pastor of that village was so hungry for the "Truth." He along with a number of his leaders were extremely fascinated with the story that I had told them regarding my older brother David. His sixteen years of addictions and dark bondage and ultimate deliverance from satan's grip seemed to inspire them. They must have asked me a hundred different questions during that day. Within those questions, it became quite apparent that there was a genuine spiritual battle that they had been entangled in within that village and community.

The next day, the pastor encouraged me not to remain any longer. He nervously told me that several of the "spirit men," as he called them, had become enraged at my presence in the village and were already trying to work "curses" upon me. He didn't actually say but clearly revealed his concern that my life was in danger. I did leave but not before I asked him and his leaders to gather with me for a time of prayer and intercession. I reminded them that spiritual battle is a part of the Christian life and encouraged them to not forget the Biblical promise that *God in us is stronger than satan in the world.*

I never take these kinds of events lightly, and that's a good thing. We boarded our small aircraft for a return trip back to Goroka, and within minutes were caught in a dangerous storm that seemed to come from nowhere. Our altitude had reached about five thousand feet when we found ourselves in the midst of heavy rain, wind and lightening. The young, yet experienced pilot named Richard reached over, touching my hand, and said loudly, "Please pray!"

In that same instance, I heard the engine briefly cut off with the bright orange engine "stall light" flickering. The rain was hammering us so hard that water was actually trickling in at the doors. In all of my trips by air during my time in the jungle, that was the first time that I became frightened. The pilot's instinct was to not maneuver the aircraft to the left or right; but rather, he gradually kept increasing the altitude until we were finally above the storm system.

There were jagged mountain peaks all around us that could have been easily struck without proper visual response. Thankfully, Richard rerouted us to the coast for an overnight in the town of Lae. As we recounted the last forty-eight hours, we were quite aware that this was not just a typical tropical storm. Richard asked me what I had prayed while we were in the plane in the midst of that storm.

With sober reluctance I said, "Richard, I asked God to not allow satan to win." I then reminded Richard that his actions as a pilot were in line with Scriptural thought as he chose not to drift to the left or right or descend into certain danger, but rather he chose to rise above the darkness and ultimately win the battle. We then prayerfully drifted off to sleep.

God has promised that he would never forsake us, even in what some would call the most trivial matters. When the village men had joyfully captured that huge wrangling python snake and had brought him into the heart of the village for roasting, I was pretty stunned, and it didn't seem very trivial to me. I was one of the guest's of honor, and the village was in an all out mode of celebration. They were determined to honor us with a feast of sweet potatoes, greens and a roasted python.

My first instinct was to run for the jungle, but what kind of witness would that be? I was inwardly saying, "God, enough is enough! I haven't had a bath in nearly three days. I've had very little sleep while I have been in this village community. My water is bitter from the military purification tablets. I'm weak from the equatorial heat as well as my ongoing struggle with malaria. I miss my family, and now, I have to eat snake!"

Thankfully, before I could whine any longer, they escorted me to the circle of feasting to get on with dinner. I can only tell you that the longer you chew a piece of python, the larger and chewier that piece of meat becomes.

To make matters worse. It was only a few weeks from that momentous event in that village when I actually stumbled over a python skin that had been shed overnight at the foot of our small porch and steps at the rear of our house in Goroka. I had risen early that morning and was making my way to the Goroka airstrip before dawn and discovered that twelve-foot long snakeskin. Our kids had been playing around those steps in our backyard the day before.

Numerous images of that far away jungle island will always remain in my mind. The image of my entrance into that remote coastal village was unforgettable. I had just walked from the airstrip that had been hewn by the village men with their machetes into the village. That's when my brain could not compute what my eyes were staring at. A young mother was just standing there with a huge smile upon her face. She was nursing an infant on one breast and a small piglet on the other breast. It was the joyful sounds of the people that brought me back to my senses. In fact, it looked as though the whole village had come out to welcome us. I had been told that most of the young children had never seen a "white man" since their birth.

How about the time that I was in a town center church as the guest preacher and just could not keep my concentration on my message? Well, what's a preacher to do when a three-year-old smacking his mother's bare breasts like he's playing some kind of game distracts him? Or how about the church service I'm preaching in, when the infant has been handed down the row of women for a brief stop to nurse on each one of their breasts? You talk about caring for one another. Then there was that shocking day when my two young national secretaries who were in training in our headquarters office came to our door and wanted to know if we would like to join them in catching, cooking and eating the beetles that were now in season.

Another image that will always remain with me came from a heart-to-heart conversation with a twenty-year-old Papua New Guinean man. He had asked me to counsel with him as to the young lady that he wanted to marry. His first sobering question was right to the point. "Is it true that men in America buy pictures of women with naked breasts?"

After a bleak sigh, I simply replied, "Yes, it is true that many men in America buy pictures of naked women." Following several seconds of silence, he then revealed his heart. "Brother, my woman is making me crazy." I then replied, "I don't understand."

He then clearly said, "The more clothes that she puts on, the more lustful my heart becomes." In my mind I was quickly thinking, "Okay, now let me get this straight. Men in America are battling lust pertaining to nude women, while men in Papua New Guinea, who see the bare breasts of women every day, are struggling with lust when these women are putting more clothes on. Hmm! I do think I'm about crazy myself!"

Well, thankfully, I snapped out of my dazed mind and was quickened by the Holy Spirit with a response to this hurting young man. We dialogued for over an hour about the "spirit of lust" that was obviously at work in both men and women, clothed or not. We prayed together for God's strength to resist our enemy at every level.

I am so grateful for the hundreds of opportunities for spiritual growth and maturity within my own life during that season of ministry in Papua New Guinea. The daily challenge of memorizing at least five new "Pidgin English" words, the most common language amongst the Papua New Guineans, to increase my ability to at least carry on personal conversations was difficult for me. Continually learning to labor for the Lord within the boundaries of unfamiliar customs was not easy, either.

Spending significant time with the national and missionary leaders while endeavoring to maintain my responsibilities as a husband and father at home were a daily challenge. Then to mesh all of that together with the continual growing weakness within my physical body due to the affects of malaria that had beleaguered me during most of my time on that island was at times overwhelming. However, I did find comfort and peace as I continued to witness a daily measure of success in "passing the torch" to those future leaders and patriarchs of that Papua New Guinean Church.

Claudia and I were all smiles when we were invited for a thirty-day ministry tour across the neighboring continent of Australia. A number of our missionary families were citizens of both Australia and New Zealand and had given positive reports about this new field director and the season of change that was transpiring in Papua New Guinea. It was one of the highest honors of my life to take my family by jet and rental car across that unique country. We traveled and gave a good report to fourteen different churches representing three separate affiliations, from Sydney on the east coast, to Adelaide in the central region, all the way to Perth on the west coast.

Valerie was nearly overwhelmed when she got to hold a newborn baby kangaroo while feeding it a bottle of milk. It had been rescued from a fatal blow to its mother by a car on the highway. She breathlessly talked about that to anyone who would listen over the next year. Our children were also very excited to get to watch some television again while staying in a number of hotels and homes. One of our sad family catch phrases was "No TV in PNG."

You would have chuckled too if you had seen how Angela and Valerie clapped their hands with joy when they saw a McDonalds in Sydney and a Burger King in Perth. Upon our arrival back in Papua New Guinea, I shared a comical story of one of our experiences with one of our Australian missionary couples. I told them about how, while we were driving into Perth, how quickly we turned that rental car into that Kentucky Fried Chicken parking lot when we spotted it. I then headed in to place our order for take-out so that we could enjoy it back at our hotel. When I had specifically asked for one portion of our order to be "all dark meat," the young lady on the other side of the counter responded with, "Sir, unlike America, all of our chickens have white meat only." Well, she definitely picked up on what many Australians called my "Yankee" dialect. However, she definitely floored me with that "white meat only" statement. I just said, "Okay, please give me a bunch of that fried 'white meat'." Our Australian missionary friends responded with, "Tim Kelton, you would find one of our Australian 'twits'!'" We all laughed.

However, the constant display of growing weakness in my body often stole the smiles and laughter from not only our family, but also our fellow colleagues. Several of our leaders had expressed their concern for my declining health. One of the national leaders tearfully advised me to return to America before it was too late.

After so many prayers and intercessions in my behalf, and only seeing continued deterioration in my strength, I knew that our time of ministry within Papua New Guinea was coming to a close. Thankfully, we had been faithful to our assignment in making every effort to lift up the name of Jesus Christ wherever we had traveled as well as "passing the torch" of spiritual leadership into the hands of capable men and women who would follow us.

It was a very sobering day when I sat in the office of that New Zealand doctor as he revealed to me his latest finding. He had diagnosed me with what he termed "malignant malaria," the most lethal type of malaria. He clearly warned me that I should return to my homeland while I was still able, or his fear was that I would return "in a box."

As Claudia and I were prayerfully and somberly in the midst of making the decision to submit our resignation to the Mission Headquarters Office in Los Angeles, she revealed some-thing that had been stirring inside her heart. "Tim, when we go back to America, we are headed to Waynesboro, Virginia." I just looked at her with bewilderment and replied, "Why Waynes-boro, Virginia?" She just gently responded, "I don't know why, but that's what I feel."

We had been to Waynesboro, Virginia, before during a time of ministry, but that particular town and community had never even entered my mind as a future home for our family. Oh well, we both sighed and committed our future once again to God's leadership.

Presently, however, we had decided to tender our resigna-tion. I had only served two years under appointment as Field Director. Our original target had been at least three years and possibly five if we were needed to stay longer. My personal dis-appointment was immense. There were still so many goals that had not been reached and so many conflicts that needed more time to resolve. The look of disappointment on the faces of the missionary personnel as well as the national leaders was punish-ing. I truly felt that I had let all of them down.

However, as our final weeks in Papua New Guinea came to an end, the Lord replaced the bitter sorrow and disappointment with a true sense of peace. We were watching these Godly lead-ers throw back their shoulders and accept more responsibility than they had ever imagined. We had been a part of this critical time of transition, and we, too, could hold our heads high.

When the Missions Headquarters Office had summoned Dr. Mason Hughes and his wife to fly from their new home in Singapore back to Papua New Guinea for a week of assessment as to the circumstances of our leaving, we were surprised. Yet we understood their concern and welcomed this special couple.

After he spent quality time with both the missionary leaders as well as the national leadership in surveying the landscape of where that Papua New Guinean Foursquare Church was currently postured as to both the present and the future, he then made his way to our home for one final visit. I can only say that Dr. Hughes final and personal words to Claudia and I brought us much comfort and calm in this storm that we had been working our way through. He made it clear that we had accomplished more in those two years in "passing the torch" of leadership to the National Church than what he felt anyone would have accomplished in a period of five years.

It was a very emotional goodbye on the day of our departure. Many of those brothers and sisters in Christ who had become good friends had tearfully gathered at the Goroka airstrip to see us off. As we climbed the steps to board that Air Nuigini Jet, there was an abundance of tearful shouts of "goodbye" and "God be with you!" Those are images that will always be with us.

Chapter 14

DON'T GIVE UP YOUR DREAMS

*"For our light affliction, which is but for a moment,
is working for us a far more exceeding
and eternal weight of glory, while we do not
look at the things which are seen,
but at the things which are not seen.
For the things which are seen are temporary,
but the things which are not seen are eternal."*
II Corinthians 4:17,18

After nearly two weeks of debriefing with the Missions Headquarters Department of our denomination in Los Angeles, we submitted our resignation as missionary personnel. This didn't come about the way that we had originally envisioned, but because of my declining health and struggling spirit, it was the correct decision.

We now had our eyes set on seeing our families. We departed Los Angeles International Airport, touching down briefly in Denver and then finished our journey by air, where we had originally began two years earlier, Indianapolis, Indiana. Claudia's family was joyfully and tearfully awaiting our arrival.

With no clear direction as to our future in the ministry, coupled with the struggles that we were experiencing in our health, we submitted to Claudia's parent's invitation to move in with them. Her folks were kindhearted people and truly displayed their love for our family. We enrolled Angela and Valerie into the local New Castle school system, and I began looking for employment as we prayerfully sought God's will as to our next step.

After several months of living in New Castle, Indiana, a momentous telephone call came from a close friend. Pastor Arlen, from Waynesboro, Virginia, extended an invitation to us to move to his town situated in the heart of the beautiful Shenandoah Valley. He and his congregation offered to rent an apartment for our family and assist me in getting a job while we were seeking God's will for future direction. I immediately recalled Claudia's words to me six months prior to that moment while our feet were still on Papua New Guinean soil as she distinctly said, "Tim, when we go back to America, we are headed to Waynesboro, Virginia."

Even today, at the time of the publishing of this book, we remain indebted to Pastor Arlen, his wife Margaret and the Waynesboro Foursquare Gospel Church family that loved and cared for us at a most critical time in our lives and ministry. It is a debt that we can never repay.

We made the move from Indiana to Virginia the day after Thanksgiving, 1983, with the assistance of my brother David and his wife Brinda. The two-bedroom apartment was a welcome sight as we slowly unpacked many of our belongings once again. Most of our personal things were still locked up in the barrels that we had shipped to that south pacific island and then two years later shipped them back to the United States. They were now sitting in storage.

Well, with our daughters enrolled in a brand new school, Jonathan stirring around as a typical two-and-a-half-year-old toddler and Claudia enjoying some of the comforts of home, I was looking for a job, desiring to make enough money to take care of us. What an exciting day it was for me when I drove with Pastor Arlen to a small Christian radio station located in Churchville, Virginia. He had heard that they were looking for another announcer.

I will never be able to thank the Lord enough for opening that door of ministry for me. The very day that they interviewed me, they hired me. I was to replace an older announcer and begin training immediately. They had just built new studios a mile up the road from the old studios and would be making the transition in less than two weeks. It was my tremendous privilege to be the first announcer "on air" in the beautiful new studios. My assignment was to be the first host of the brand new *Sonrise Show*, playing light contemporary Christian music.

WNLR-1150 AM first began with a unique young man named Marc. I still remember the billboard in the heart of Staunton, Virginia, with his face posing a silly grin and the invitation for the community to tune into the radio show with "The King's Kid." Then later came the older announcer and his morning show called "Eggs and bacon with Burt."

For nearly two years I was honored to host the *Sonrise Show*. My health had improved a little, and I was very grateful to have this small part in the ministry of Christian radio that was touching thousands of lives every day. However, I was continually struggling with the reality that I had served as a pastor for eleven years in Charlotte followed by two years as Field Director and missionary in Papua New Guinea. While I would be asked to preach from time to time in the Waynesboro Foursquare Gospel Church, I was inwardly hurting, as I was keenly aware that I was not fulfilling the pastoral call upon my life. Those feelings were intensified when I was faced with not making enough money at the radio station to take care of my family.

We had moved from that apartment to a small but beautiful house in a neighboring community called Stuarts Draft, Virginia. The Lord had opened a door for us to purchase this house. We felt at peace about the decision, but the finances were more and more a struggle. While some of our friends and colleagues felt that we were out of God's will, we kept sensing that God had called us to this beautiful valley in the heart of Virginia.

Many of those friends were really upset when they heard that I had resigned my position at the Christian radio station and had taken a job at one of the local factories. I was now working twelve-hour shifts during the night as a packing inspector for a vinyl siding company; however, we were now better able to take care of ourselves.

I was totally stunned at the numerous opportunities of ministry that God opened to me during those thirteen months in that factory. After learning that I was a Christian and pastor and even a missionary, individual after individual would ask me for advice and counsel as to their marriage relationships. Many were the times that I was asked to pray with them over the various problems that were holding them in bondage. Some of the men actually came to our home for counsel and help. It was truly an amazing time of personal, one-on-one ministry, and it was stirring up the pastoral gift once again within me.

At that point, Claudia and I made a monumental decision in our lives. Believing that God had brought us to the Shenandoah Valley and hoping to once again fulfill our pastoral call while desiring not to bring tension to either of the local Foursquare

Churches, we withdrew from the Foursquare Denomination and began the process of pioneering an independent church located in our hometown of Stuarts Draft. However, in spite of our best intention and objective, unease did arise among some of our friends and colleagues, and it was understandable. Some perceived that we were in some rebellious mode while others simply felt that we had now completely moved out of God's will for our lives. Yet we simply kept praying that any discord and misunderstanding of our decision would quickly subside so that we could just simply serve our Lord as we had endeavored to do over the past fifteen years. Nevertheless, in less than a year, Tim and Claudia would be facing a far more severe conflict within our lives.

I will never forget the frightening moment of being carried out of our basement bedroom by the local rescue squad. The lights overhead faded as those professionals quickly loaded me on a stretcher in to the ambulance and hurried off to the Waynesboro Hospital Emergency Room. Claudia was horrified at the sight of the blood oozing from my mouth. I was nearly unconscious.

I was in the hospital for twenty-two days as local physicians along with their colleagues at the University of Virginia Medical Center located across the Blue Ridge Mountains in Charlottesville, endeavored to diagnose what was going on. They finally began to dialogue with Claudia and I about their discoveries and painful prognosis. We were both stunned.

While lying in the hospital bed one of those twenty-two days, I asked my personal physician, Dr. Wesley J. Ross, to pray with me. I knew that he was a strong Christian. It was a moment that I will never forget when he sat on the edge of the bed and joined hands with me. We audibly agreed together in prayer for God's wisdom and leadership over my situation.

On the day before Thanksgiving, 1986, as we wearily sat before a team of specialists in Internal Medicine at the university hospital, they emotionally revealed their thinking. They were convinced that I was dying and there was nothing that could be done to stop it. They understood the battle that I had faced since the early 1980s that resulted from the "malignant malaria" that struck me while in the jungles of Papua New Guinea. They had now connected that dreaded disease that had been lurking within my body for several years with what they concluded was some kind of additional contamination from either bad water or food while in those jungles.

They clearly described the large number of Viet Nam Veterans that had died from this very disease. They understood that I was not a war veteran with a history in Viet Nam, but the environmental circumstances were the same in that Papua New Guinean jungle. As they described the deadly vascular disease called "Wegener's Granulomatosis," they spoke of only ninety days of life remaining for me.

On my final day under doctor's care several months later, Dr. Carol Brunner, one of the leading physicians of Internal Medicine at the University of Virginia Medical Center, spoke words that I will never forget. "Mr. Kelton, I have talked about you with my husband while at my dinner table. I told him that our case file was thick pertaining to your set of circumstances, clearly demonstrating that you should not be alive." She continued, "I told him that you refused to die and that your personal faith had played a major role in the final results." She then readjusted her eyeglasses and gently smiled as she concluded, "Mr. Kelton, I have no doubt but that you are gradually being cured." With that overwhelming statement from a medical professional, I slowly made my way down the hallway, out of the door and into my car.

When people hear of this dark moment within our lives and then inquire as to why I am still among the living, my single reply is, "It was not my time to go home to be with the Lord." I credit the prayers of hundreds, maybe thousands of people that held me before the throne of God as well as my own personal resolve deep within me. That tenacity came from the still quiet voice of God while I lay in the Critical Care Unit of the hospital. In the midst of all the turmoil and struggle at that perilous moment, I heard this word very clearly deep within me: "Tim, do everything that you can do, then leave the rest with Me."

I had been at death's door several times in my life as a result of numerous events, but this episode seemed the most ominous. I wasn't afraid, but I understood clearly that my lifelong enemy, satan, had come to take me out. Once again, I also clearly understood that *I owed the God of the Bible a debt that I could never repay.* While I have lived these past twenty years with significant damage done to the muscles in my lower legs and ankles, an ongoing affect of that killer disease, I have been enabled in many various and sundry ways to continue to touch my world for the cause of Christ.

It was during that time of recovery that I received a telephone call requesting that I meet two friends for lunch. As I sat with Allan and Rusty, I was nearly overwhelmed at what they were saying to me. They were offering me employment once again at that special Christian radio station that I deeply loved, WNLR-1150 AM-New Life Radio. However, this time they were not only requesting that I return as the morning announcer and host of the *Sonrise Show*, but that I would take on the responsibility of Operations Manager as well. I was thrilled at the invitation but was very nervous as to the ongoing weakness within my physical body.

It was a joyful season for me personally. I understood that God had gifted me with the ability to communicate and labor for Him within the Christian media. I have never taken that special gift and anointing lightly.

One of the great highlights of that time was when I along with some of our radio staff participated in the Washington For Jesus gathering in our nation's capitol. Several hundred thousand believers came from all across the country in order to join together in prayer for America. I interviewed a number of the guest speakers and musicians at that tremendous gathering so that we could broadcast their thoughts to our radio audience back in Virginia at a later date. Some of those interviews included Christian singers Michael W. Smith and Steve Green, along with well-known individuals such as Rosie Grier, Peter Marshall and Beverly LaHaye. This great and historical day was on my 40th birthday, April 29, 1988.

Another great focal point for me during that time of ministry was in regard to an invitation that I had received to share my personal testimony on the *PTL Club*. The *PTL Ministry*, based in Fort Mill, South Carolina, was doing everything that they could do to overcome the tragedy of failures and subsequent imprisonment of its founder, Jim Bakker. That period of time had been devastating to literally tens of thousands of Christians across America.

As I sat under those bright television lights in the central studio at Heritage USA, sharing my recent testimony of God's protection over my life during that past year, I couldn't help but smile as I understood that this "live" telecast was being simulcast on our local Christian radio station nearly three hundred miles away in the central Shenandoah Valley.

Upon my return to Virginia, I was overwhelmed at the response of our listening audience. That next morning back in the radio studios during the *Sonrise Show*, the telephone calls just would not cease as people were joyfully and tearfully thanking me and the radio station management for making such a unique event possible.

I was also amazed at the array of invitations for ministry that I was receiving. It was humbling to step into the pulpits of so many various denominations. In one short period of time, I had shared my personal testimony at Calvary Baptist Church, Christian Missionary Alliance, First Church of God, Faith Christian, Loch Willow Presbyterian, Hopeman Parkway Church of God, White Hill Church of the Brethren and a local chapter of Cowboys For Christ, all located within a relative short distance of each other in the midst of the Shenandoah Valley. Two resident columnists, Mary Pitman and Mildred Gleason, requested interviews with me for articles to be highlighted and featured in local newspapers. Another great honor was when I accepted the invitation to serve as one of several advisors to a local Women's Aglow chapter.

However, as a result of the continued invitations for me to minister in numerous churches up and down the east coast and after only a year and a half back on the radio, I submitted my resignation to the management. In spite of this painful decision for me personally, I was simply trying once again to follow what I sensed was God's will for my life.

The next thirty months were an incredible time of ministry for me. While it meant that I would be separated from Claudia and the children frequently, it continued to birth and establish the truth that reverberates within me this very day, *God in you can change the world.*

My childhood dream had been that I would preach in all 50 states of America within my lifetime. Well, that hasn't happened yet, but in that brief season of just over two years I was privileged to minister in *two* cities in Alabama; *eight* cities in Florida; *six* cities in Georgia; *four* cities in South Carolina; *nineteen* cities in North Carolina; *fifteen* cities in Virginia; *three* cities in West Virginia; *two* cities in Pennsylvania; *nine* cities in Ohio; and *five* cities in Indiana.

Some of those invitations were for a single service. Many were for three or four days of ministry. In all, 73 towns and cities, including 10 different denominations and 5 Christian television stations, opened their doors to me, a simple but committed man that had surrendered his life to the purposes of God, in spite of three generations of atheism and witchcraft that had preceded me. The God of the Bible deserves and receives the glory for such a testimony.

One of my most mind boggling invitations was from a young man that grew up during our eleven year pastoral ministry in Charlotte. His parents, David and Barbara, were unique individuals that had brought us much encouragement during that pastoral season. Their only child Dennis was communicating with me as to his extraordinary request.

"Pastor Tim, I was just a little guy when we started coming to your church. I want you to be the one to marry Lorrie and me, but it's going to be unusual." I was thinking, "My whole life has been unusual, Dennis." He continued, "We want to have the wedding ceremony at *Carowinds Amusement Park*. That's where we first met."

His voice was distinctly nervous as he pressed on. "We've already checked it all out, and the management is excited about it. It will be their first wedding at the park. We want the wedding ceremony to be in the main walkway across from the candy store where we first saw each other." As usual in my life and ministry, I was unable to find the simple word "no." Their dream came true on that historic September day. They are now the proud parents of three great sons of their own.

One additional thrill and privilege for me during that brief season of ministry was an invitation to produce a daily radio program on my favorite Christian radio station in the Shenandoah Valley. The new General Manager of WNLR, Tom Watson, along with his Program Director, Russ Whitesell, opened the door for me to produce and air a daily 15-minute teaching program.

Those two tenderhearted men allowed me the opportunity to touch the large community of listeners to Christian radio in the Shenandoah Valley for the cause of Jesus Christ. The daily program was entitled, *The Deeper Life* and aired at 10 a.m. every weekday morning for that year, and that was without cost to me personally. I will never be able to repay them for that generous gift to this minister of the Gospel.

Tim and Claudia Kelton had now come to another significant moment in their lives. Our new District Supervisor, Glenn Burris, Jr., had asked us to take a pastoral assignment in Covington, Virginia. It was an independent charismatic congregation seeking affiliation with our Foursquare Denomination and was currently without a pastor. There was a definite sense within us that we should prayerfully take this assignment.

I traveled weekly back and forth from our home in Stuarts Draft to Covington. We were awaiting the end of the current school year so as not to distress both Valerie and Jonathan with our move. Our oldest daughter Angela was now attending Bridgewater College. We put our home up for sale and fully moved to the town of Covington. Our heart as pastors has always been that your assignment as a pastor is for life, unless God moves you on.

One of my greatest privileges as pastor of the Good News Foursquare Church was to help develop and initiate a ministry within the local jails and prisons within that general area. Part of that mission evolved as a result of a young man named Ethan. He had recently been released from serving time in prison. He was hungry to serve the Lord and truly desired to help inmates.

Our hearts meshed together almost immediately. I became a father image and mentor to this young man. He responded prayerfully and humbly as we saw door after door open to our unique ministry within the jails and prisons.

I will never forget the inmate that wept before us as he described his decision to commit fraud within his administrative position of a local waste management company. He kept saying to us, "If I could only take those five minutes back," the five-minute space in which he had made and acted upon his criminal decision. He would serve a decade behind bars for that single act. We would pray with him every week during our visit to the Allegany County Jail.

There was an inmate in the Clifton Forge Jail that really got to me. He had been arrested in Florida and served time there and was now serving time for bank fraud in Virginia. He would soon be released to an Ohio prison in order to pay for his past crimes in that state. It boggled my mind as to how this young man in his mid twenties had so many different criminal files and court decisions already against him.

I first noticed him when I would stick my hand through the bars and endeavor to shake each of the inmates' hands. He would always move to the rear of the cell and just stare at me. Sometimes I would wave or smile directly at him, but always without any response from him.

After several months of ministry within that lock-up, he finally responded one day. He shook my hand through the bars and simply said, "I've been watching you. I wanted to see if you and your black brother were for real." He then shared his story of being raised in church in Ohio, and his practice of reading his Bible and singing Christian songs.

Then one dark and treacherous day in his young life, he decided to commit a criminal act. He wasn't immediately caught and thus began his numerous episodes of breaking the law in numerous states. Then came the day of reckoning when he was apprehended and was now going to serve more than 30 years of his life behind bars.

He wept openly before us. He said that he had repented before God and had found forgiveness but his heart was breaking over what he had done to his parents. He described to us how they had both aged as a result of all that he put them through. His plea to us was to help him deal with the pain and sorrow that he had brought upon his mother and father.

Over the remainder of that year, before his release back to his home state to serve decades behind bars, we earnestly prayed with him during our weekly visits. Upon our final visit a few days before his departure, he spoke just a few simple words that neither Ethan nor I would ever forget, "You have saved my life." With tears in all of our eyes, we prayed that God's grace and mercy would help each of us to remain faithful in our relationship with Christ and that someday we would be together once again.

In spite of the success of this type of ministry and the growing love that both Claudia and I had developed toward this congregation we were once again sensing that we were not the permanent pastors for this congregation. The stress of not being able to sell our house in Stuarts Draft had been very frustrating to us as well. We had dropped the sale price five different times over the space of one year in hopes of selling the house to a number of interested families, but nothing would seem to work out.

After meeting Pastor Jim and his wife Jan, and hearing their passion for the pastoral ministry, we sensed that we had once again accomplished our assignment in helping to pass the torch of leadership to capable and gifted leaders. Our denomination released us from our assignment to Covington, Virginia. So once again we packed our belongings and moved; however, this time we did have a house to go back to.

We had no more than returned back to Stuarts Draft when the new pastor of the Waynesboro Foursquare Church made a visit to our house. Pastor Joe detailed a number of his objectives in leading this church into the future, and he made it quite clear that he was hoping that we would join him in this spiritual venture. With little hesitation, we consented to his offer. To our joyful surprise, we would once again join hands with another couple in which we had been privileged to be their pastors during our eleven years in Charlotte. Pastor Roger and his wife Jo would also move to the area and serve as the new administrator over the church.

Over the next two years, I would serve this growing congregation on the pastoral staff. One of my major responsibilities would be in the area of pastoral counseling. I would also take the leadership over the new Shenandoah Bible Institute. As the Director of SBI, it would not only be my joy to teach, but I was to help write the curriculum for serious study of the Bible. I was thrilled to see people from many denominations enroll in the night classes.

However, my greatest challenge was my assignment as the leader of the senior high school young people, a friendly youth group numbering about thirty. I was very apprehensive as to a forty-five year-old like myself leading this group of teens. In all honesty, I left no stone unturned. I challenged those bright youth on nearly every subject, and at times they would stiffen their jaws in resistance, but in the end the Lord gave me favor with them.

One of the most fruitful times was during a three-month period where I challenged them about the kind of music that they were listening to. I made a deal with them. I told them to bring in their favorite cassettes or CDs, and we as a group would listen to their favorite song. We would then replay it, stopping the song every few words and make sure that everyone clearly understood what they were listening to. Then in return, I would bring in my favorite contemporary Christian songs, and we would do the same. It was like a music swap, their song, then my song, then another of their songs and then another of mine. The hour would go by fast.

They were greatly stunned as they actually learned of the harsh, abrasive, sexually explicit and risqué words within many of the popular secular songs that had been their favorites. I was deeply moved, as many of the parents would privately convey their gratitude to me for this unusual manner of teaching their teens. Even many years later, I have heard positive words pertaining to those three vital months on the subject of music from some of those past youth who are now grown up and married, and some with their own children. Once again, I could clearly see the truth, that *God in me could change the world.*

Another major event with those teens was when we packed up two vans and several cars and headed across the Blue Ridge Mountains to Liberty University in Lynchburg, Virginia. Thousands of high school and college students had gathered for a three hour musical concert with the well-known Christian group, Newsboys, along with a newer group called Audio Adrenaline. That huge auditorium was rockin' with Christian music. Afterwards, our teens gave me high fives all the way to the vans and cars. My ears were ringing for at least a week.

That very fruitful season of ministry while on the pastoral staff of the Waynesboro Foursquare Church came to an end on Sunday, December 2, 1995. That was the very first Sunday worship of our newest pastoral assignment, Maranatha! Foursquare Church of Stuarts Draft, Virginia. We are now in our eleventh year as pastors of this unique and exceptional congregation. Our determination has been to plant a church within the community in which we have lived and raised our three children since our return from the mission field of Papua New Guinea in 1983. We have moved from a middle school auditorium to an empty florist shop, then temporarily to our home and are now meeting at the Solid Rock Café Youth Center. We fully plan to purchase property for the construction of a church sanctuary and ministry facility. All within the Lord's perfect timing. As we have continually learned, *timing with God is everything.*

Every Sunday, it is my privilege to look into the faces of people that come from many different backgrounds. They come from a mixture of both broken and stable homes. Many have suffered broken marriages themselves and are seeking healing and restoration for their own personal lives. Many have started their own families and are determined to establish strong, stable Christian homes. They are witnessing on their jobs and in their communities. It has been one of the greatest pleasures of my life to be the pastor of these unwavering believers.

Chapter 15

FOLLOW THE LEADER

"Behold, children are a heritage from the Lord,
the fruit of the womb is a reward.
Like arrows in the hand of a warrior, so are the children of one's youth."
Psalm 127:3,4

Our first born, Angela Sue, was standing alongside me in that grocery store line. She was about four years of age on that notable day. The gentleman directly in front of us had just finished emptying his cart at the cash register for checkout. Unfortunately, Angela was never known for quiet speech when she would speak her opinions. That small girl with pig tails then resounded, "Oh, Daddy! He's got some nasty beer!"

The man quickly turned his head toward us as his eyes focused on Angela. He then somberly looked up at me. I gently said, "I'm sorry, sir." He immediately replied, "No, don't be sorry. She's right." He then paid the clerk, gathered up his purchase and departed.

Before the day of stringent laws pertaining to seatbelts and special safety seats for children in automobiles, Angela was riding between Claudia and I in the front seat of our car. We were on our way somewhere, when we decided that this was as good a time as any for our special announcement. Claudia softly stated, "Angela, we are going to have another baby." Angela's mouth immediately popped open as she quickly turned her head toward me and nervously responded, "What are you going to do with me, Daddy, throw me away?" Well, we simultaneously responded with numerous emotional and tearful words trying to comfort our little one with the knowledge that she was safe and secure with her mommy and daddy.

There is a picture in one of our various photo albums that highlights our historic first night on the South Pacific Island of Papua New Guinea. After months of packing and preparation and then saying emotional good-byes to family and friends in America, we were finally there, ten thousand miles away from America and hoping for a successful transition to our new home.

Exhausted and worn out, Angela and Valerie had snuggled up together in one bed and fallen asleep. They had told us that they were afraid to sleep in their separate beds. The dark circles under both of their eyes leaped out at this somber father as I snapped that picture.

Many years later, as a high school teen, Angela asked me if she could talk with me about something. I will never forget her emotional words as she described to me the scene in one of her classes that day. As a result of some kind of open dialogue within that class, Angela discovered that she was the only student in that particular class that did not have divorced parents. She detailed the collective questions and statements from her classmates that finally revealed the one defining conclusion of that historic moment, that "Angie's dad is her real dad, and her mother is her real mother." As she stood from where we were both seated, she softly kissed my cheek and tearfully said, "Dad, it had never even entered my mind to thank you and Mom for loving each other and staying together."

In the not too distant future, we would be holding hands as we stood together in the stairwell just a few steps from the foyer of the First Baptist Church of Waynesboro, Virginia. This day was her wedding day. She was nervously and anxiously awaiting the moment of walking down that aisle and taking the hands of Richard Beadles, her husband to be. She had specifically asked me to just be her dad on that momentous day. Not a preacher, not a pastor, not a missionary, not a radio or television personality; "Just be my dad." However, she did want me to read Paul's "love letter" to the Corinthian believers on that very extraordinary day.

Our second born, Valerie Lynne, had quite a reputation in her early childhood years. More than one individual had asked me if I had ever seen her just "simply walk." At first, I hadn't really thought that much about it, but I did begin to take note. Our family and friends were correct in their assessment of this lively little girl. She rarely walked and almost always skipped or hopped to wherever she was headed to. It was amazing and amusing to watch.

Another area in which Valerie was truly amazing, but I can tell you not so amusing, was her artistry skills. She was a natural born artist, delightfully following in the footsteps of her very artistic mother, Claudia. The only problem in her younger years was that she would consistently produce many of her colorful portraits on her bedroom walls. I can only tell you that when we resigned from our first pastoral assignment in Charlotte and vacated the parsonage in preparation of moving overseas, I was forced to make a trip to the local Sherwin Williams paint store and seek their advice on how to successfully cover up Valerie's manifold portraits that kept bleeding through the paint that I was currently using. They did finally direct me to a "specialty paint" for such conditions.

That final service at the First Foursquare Church in Charlotte, where we had been pastoring for eleven years, was a solemn service for us. At that moment, we didn't actually know that we were headed to the South Pacific, but we had been notified that we were one of three families that had been positioned through the selection process for assignments overseas.

Emotions were running high as church members, friends and some of our family had gathered that day to say goodbye to us. Angela, age seven, as far as we could determine was dealing with it as well as possible. However, we were unprepared for the tearful scene that was before us with our three-and-half-year-old sweetheart, Valerie.

When one of the men in the church had come and whispered in my ear that I should immediately follow him, he portrayed a sense of urgency. As we made our way out of the church sanctuary and into the parking lot, he led me around the corner of the building. There stood my precious little lady weeping.

It was a visual scene that I will never forget. Valerie had placed her back against the cedar siding walls of the church building with each arm extended against the walls and was audibly crying. When I and several other members of the church quickly rushed to her side, we were all in tears. She looked at me and painfully said, "Daddy, I don't want to leave. This is our church, Daddy, why do we have to go?"

To this day, I am so grateful that I was unable to give her any kind of an answer, an answer that could have potentially planted the wrong seed down in her fragile spirit. I just wrapped my arms around her while picking her up and, holding her close, making it crystal clear that her mommy and daddy would always love her no matter what.

About a year or so from that tearful moment, after our arrival in Papua New Guinea, Valerie and one of her Papua New Guinean friends emotionally came running to the window at the side of the house in order to get Claudia's attention. After they had successfully covered Valerie with wet, muddy, black dirt from head to toe, Valerie joyfully shouted, "Look Mommy, I'm a Papua New Guinean now!" What else could a shocked and chuckling mother do but hurry to get a washcloth and towel and start the process of cleaning up that little American/Papua New Guinean lady?

Two decades later, it was my great privilege to stand front and center in the special Grand Ballroom of the Ingleside Resort in Verona, Virginia, on Valerie's wedding day. What a memory for me as I watched that beautiful and nervous bride, escorted by her six-foot-five-inch baby brother, make their way to the front of the ballroom. It would be Jonathan's special and unique privilege to join his sister's hands with Jeremy Kong, her husband-to-be.

With a different mind set than her sister Angela, before this momentous day, Valerie had said to me, "Dad, you are the only pastor that I have ever had. That's why you should be the one that leads our wedding ceremony." So, with a thankful heart that I was able to be a part of both of my daughters weddings, however they would each decide, I did my best that very important day to tie that marriage knot, as tight as I possibly could.

Our third born, Jonathan Paul, had been given a tremendous task for a newborn, and there was nothing that he could do about it. He would become the focus of many family members, friends and medical physicians. It was difficult enough for everyone to release our two young daughters to go live in a country that lacked both medical personnel and facilities meeting modern day standards, but to take a newborn baby to such conditions brought a tremendous amount of criticism upon Claudia and I as well as our denomination. In all truthfulness, I couldn't find any appropriate response that would satisfy the critics.

During our season of ministry on that jungle island, I worked hard to keep a steady flow of current pictures of our children, regularly air mailed to our family back in the United States. During many of our dinners around our small table, we would also make audio recordings on cassette tapes of our family talking, giving individual updates and sometimes even singing some of the new Pidgin English songs that we had been learning.

Of course, in the early months, not much noise was coming from Jonathan, but it always brought a smile to our faces when we would ask one of the girls to describe what their baby brother was wearing and then give a finger-by-finger, arm-by-arm, leg-by-leg update on how he was looking. In six months or so, baby Jonathan started making himself known on the audio-letters by his own unique squeaks, groans, and noises.

Jonathan had become very sick and was losing weight each day. It was a frightening time for us. Many people around the world had joined us in intercessory prayer for our young son. In time, God answered those sincere prayers, and Jonathan began to gradually recover.

One of the characteristics of that young toddler a year later was when he would do his best to mimic his father, especially when we as a family were in a public setting, like a church service or some conference that I would be invited to. One of our favorite snapshots of Jonathan is when he was standing right next to his dad and shaking hands with dozens of Papua New Guinean leaders and their wives, just like his dad. In the coming months, it became very clear to anyone watching, that the hundreds of Papua New Guineans that would make their way through the line in order to shake the hand of Tim Kelton, their Field Director, were much more interested in shaking the hand of the little blond-haired son that stood right beside him.

A short time from that day, upon our arrival back in the United States, we as a family made our way to the Los Angeles Zoo. What an enjoyable time we were having, but something unexpected and quite remarkable occurred while we were slowly making our way through some of the jungle settings. All three of our children displayed an unusual quietness about them. It then became apparent to Claudia and I that they were all of a sudden mentally reliving the past two years within the jungle setting of Papua New Guinea.

Then to top that off, Jonathan, who was seated in a stroller, started reaching and calling out to a large number of folks that were also making their way through this jungle setting. They joyfully responded to that little white boy with blond hair by shaking his hand and gently talking with him. They were all black. They were quite surprised at his reaction to them, and one of the men came to my side and verbalized his emotion.

He said, "In all of my years, I have never had any white person act so joyfully toward me, a black man." His mouth quickly opened in surprise when I told him that we had just returned from two years in Papua New Guinea.

Years later, I will never forget the emotion that Jonathan and I exuded when he sheepishly made his way out of the side door of the Stuarts Draft High School basketball gymnasium and climbed into my Dodge Ram Van and boyishly said, "Dad, I made the varsity basketball team." We gave each other high fives as we tearfully pondered the decision of Coach Cochran, inviting a freshman to the ranks of the varsity players.

It was another significant day within the Kelton family when Jonathan was standing at the front of the Light House Church, in the rural community of Churchville, Virginia, and awaited the doors of that beautiful sanctuary to open, revealing his lovely bride, Katie Keeler. With his two brothers-in-law, Richard and Jeremy, and one of his best friends, Jay, standing beside him, Jonathan's emotional smile was enormous as this bride and groom joined hands and turned to face this nervous father. Within that wedding ceremony I recounted the first time that I had really noticed Katie.

It was after a serious auto accident in which Jonathan had been involved in. During those subsequent weeks of recovery, Katie stood out like a bright light. In spite of all of the friends and cute girls that made there way into our house to encourage this son who was stuck in a hospital bed, Katie would consistently and quietly sit at the back of all the activity. Day after day, sometimes even silently and discreetly, she cared for some of his personal needs. I was thinking inwardly, "I don't know what girl that you will some day marry, but son, this one is a keeper."

It was definitely an extraordinary moment when I watched my son, Jonathan Kelton, carry his beautiful bride Katie, still robed in her wedding gown, to their car just as his father had done thirty-six years earlier with his beautiful bride.

Let me take us now to another whole dimension of life. For years, Claudia had communicated a specific phrase to me that in all honesty concerned me every time that I would hear her say it. She would say, "Being a grandmother is a 'sickness' that I have always wanted." However, now that I am a grandfather, I completely understand.

Our lives took on a whole new dimension on February 9, 1999, when our first grandchild, Courtney Sue Beadles, was born. I did not think it was possible for me to love any other child as much as I had loved my own, but something monumental happened when they placed that newborn baby girl into my arms. My heart nearly exploded with a new kind of love, and to my joy continues to expand to this very day.

What a privilege it was on that historic Sunday morning when this pastor and grandfather was given the leadership in this special "baby dedication" service of Courtney. I remember the deep emotion within me as I looked into the eyes of my oldest daughter, Angela, hoping to encourage her and Richard to be unified and determined in raising their child to follow Christ.

It always brings a smile when I hear Courtney lead in prayer at the dinner table. What a joy to watch her sing worship songs in the church service or go around and hug each of the members as they enter church.

Any grandparent would be in tears if they heard what I heard. Courtney was about four years old at the time. She had snuggled up on my lap when she somberly said, "Papaw, sometimes I miss you so much, I cry."

Then there was the evening that Courtney and her mother had entered their car and were about to leave our house. I had followed them out to our backyard deck in order to wave goodbye. Then it started. With the window rolled down, Courtney yelled, "I love you, Papaw!"

I waved my hand as I responded, "I love you, Courtney!" She then shouted back, "I love you!"

I answered in return, "I love you!" Courtney then nearly silenced me as she and her mother were pulling out of our driveway and were almost out of sight when she screamed, "I love you more, Papaw!" They disappeared out of sight as I tearfully waved and softly said, "I love you more, Courtney Sue Beadles."

With a smile on her face, Angela responded to me a short time after that by saying, "Dad, you are so pathetic. My five-year-old daughter, Courtney, has her hooks in you so deep that she will always get her way when she's with her Papaw." I replied, "Uh … that's not … uh … necessarily so."

Another very historic day for our family was May 6, 2003. It was the day that Valerie and Jeremy's son, Caleb Sebasjin Kong, was born. While it was a day of great joy for our family, we were all very troubled over this new born baby's condition. He was breathing so rapidly that his physicians moved him into an isolation room in order to have more freedom to try to stabilize his breathing.

After verifying that I was not just a troubled grandfather but was an ordained pastor, the nursing staff allowed me and Jeremy into that room. My heart was breaking as we postured ourselves close to that little bundle. I will never forget that scene. His little chest and mouth were moving in such rapid sequence. Watching him struggle to breathe along with the sounds of all the equipment that was hooked up to him startled me. I am so grateful for the privilege that I had on that momentous day to anoint Caleb's little forehead with oil, as his father Jeremy and I prayed together for God's touch on that brand new baby. Over the next few days Caleb's condition continued to improve, and he was released to go home. We were all rejoicing!

Let this grandfather brag just a little. Before Caleb was three, he could recite all twenty-six letters of the alphabet and count to one hundred. Of course he gets most of that from his brilliant parents Valerie and Jeremy, but I still think a little of that comes from his "Papaw and Grammy."

We pass out tambourines to the children in our church family for Sunday worship. It always brings a smile to our members when they hear Caleb pounding that tambourine. He's usually the loudest "Amen" when his "papaw/pastor" seeks an "Amen" from the congregation.

Recently Claudia was leading our church children in a lesson on rejoicing. She had gathered together some kids' musical instruments and led the kids outdoors for a "Hallelujah March." Those kids were raising their arms in praise to God while playing their instruments, and Caleb, being the youngest, didn't allow the older ones to out shout him.

The peace and satisfaction of knowing that Claudia and I have not only influenced our three precious children toward the Kingdom of God, but that we are now being given the opportunity to touch their children has been a reward nearly beyond description. Truly, *God in you can change the world!*

Let me make this statement one more time. I owe the God of the Bible a debt that I will never be able to repay; a debt for His abundant grace over my life; a debt for His abundant mercy over my family. His unfailing love has continually overshadowed my life. To God be the glory!

Conclusion

*"Jesus said to him, 'I am the way, the truth, and the life.
No one comes to the Father except through Me'."*
John 14:6

I am so grateful that you have read through this book. In all honesty,
I have wondered why anyone would want to read a portion of the life
story of a preacher; however, I have committed that to God. In fact, I
have earnestly prayed that whoever would hold this book in their hands
would by God's grace make it to this page.

I have asked God to allow me the privilege of praying with you.
The Bible says where just two or three agree together in prayer, they
can be sure that the God of the Bible is listening to their prayers. So, I
am asking you to join me in this prayer.

*"Father God, thank you for giving me the great gift of life. Help
me to take full advantage of every day that you give me. Please forgive
me for squandering those days that I have not lived according to Your
purpose and plan for my life.*

*Lord God of the Bible, today, I surrender my life's dreams and
ambitions into Your hands. I desire to fulfill Your purpose and plan for
my life. I believe that You know what's best for my life. So please, help
me to hear only Your voice as I daily yield to Your perfect will.*

*Jesus, I believe that You are God's only Son. I believe that every
sin that I have committed can be forgiven by God, as I acknowledge
this very day my regret and sorrow for those sins of my past. I believe
that Father God has made it very clear within the pages of the Bible
that all sinners are held accountable for their sins. I also believe that
You came to earth to take my failures, disobedience and sins upon Your
own perfect life. Thank You my Lord Jesus Christ that You died in my
place. That is a debt that I owe You that I will never be able to repay.
Today, I acknowledge that You, Jesus Christ, will now live within and
through me and that You are truly my personal Savior. Amen!"*

Signature: _____

Date: _____

Endnotes

[1] Garr Memorial Church, Charlotte, North Carolina.

[2] Life Pacific College, San Dimas, California.

[3] International Church of the Foursquare Gospel, General Supervisor, Los Angeles, California.

[4] "Move That Mountain," Jim Bakker with Robert Paul Lamb, Logos International, Plainfield, New Jersey, ©1976.

[5] "FORGIVEN – The Rise And Fall Of Jim Bakker And The PTL Ministry," Charles E. Shepherd, Atlantic Monthly Press, New York, New York, ©1989.

[6] Bishop John Giminez, Rock Church, Virginia Beach, Virginia.

[7] "Prensa Libre" Newspaper, Guatemala City, Guatemala, ©June 4, 1976.

[8] "Chimes," Cathedral Of Tomorrow, Cuyahoga Falls, Ohio, Sunday, March 12, 1978.

[9] "Chosen To Live," David F. Kelton with R. Russell Bixler, Whitaker House, Springdale, Pennsylvania, ©1983.1

[10] Calvary Foursquare Church, Manila, Philippines.

[11] Daesung Christian School, Taejon, South Korea.

[12] Foursquare Missions International, Director Of Missions, Los Angeles, California.

[13] University Of Virginia Medical Center, Department Of Internal Medicine, Charlottesville, Virginia.